Intercultural Competence in ELT

Yeşim Bektaş Çetinkaya (ed.)

Intercultural Competence in ELT

Raising Awareness in Classrooms

PETER LANG

**Bibliographic Information published by the
Deutsche Nationalbibliothek**
The Deutsche Nationalbibliothek lists this publication in the Deutsche
Nationalbibliografie; detailed bibliographic data is available online at
http://dnb.d-nb.de.

Library of Congress Cataloging-in-Publication Data
A CIP catalog record for this book has been applied for at the
Library of Congress.

ISBN 978-3-631-82014-8 (Print)
E-ISBN 978-3-631-82015-5 (E-PDF)
E-ISBN 978-3-631-83430-5 (EPUB)
E-ISBN 978-3-631-83431-2 (MOBI)
DOI 10.3726/b17543

© Peter Lang GmbH
Internationaler Verlag der Wissenschaften
Berlin 2020
All rights reserved.

Peter Lang – Berlin · Bern · Bruxelles · New York · Oxford · Warszawa · Wien

This publication has been peer reviewed.

www.peterlang.com

To my beloved family for their love and support

Contents

Yeşim Bektaş-Çetinkaya

Introduction: English(es) and Culture in Language Teaching

The 21st century Technological revolution has facilitated worldwide communication, and expanded personal and cultural relationships between individuals and groups on an unprecedented scale. People from different countries and backgrounds are now in constant communication. English language, the main medium of this mass communication, is increasingly taught as foreign or second language in school systems around the world. In some countries, English has undergone a nativization process (Kachru, 1992) and thus emerged in different varieties, referred as World Englishes, while in other parts of the word, such as in Europe and Southeast Asia, it is considered as Lingua Franca (Jenkins, Cogo, & Dewey, 2011; Seidlhofer, 2011).

As a result of this increased contact, in the field of English language education, the importance of developing learners' intercultural competence has been strongly emphasized (e.g. ACTFL, 2006; Byram, 1997; Byram, Gribkova, & Starkey, 2002; Council of Europe, 2001; Furstenberg, 2010). The urgent need for developing language teachers' and learners/users' intercultural competence has been voiced on both sides of the Atlantic, by national and intergovernmental organizations such as the Council of Europe, and ACTFL in the USA. One of the four ACTFL Performance Descriptors for Language Learners is identified as "Cultural Awareness", which addresses the question "How is the language learner's cultural knowledge reflected in language use?". Similarly, intercultural competence was identified as one of the key general competences for language learners in the Council of Europe's Common European Framework of Reference for Languages. The need to extend teacher knowledge through integrating intercultural aspects into practice, and into teacher education programs, has been voiced by many (Atay, 2005; Bektas-Cetinkaya, 2014; Bektas-Cetinkaya & Börkan, 2012; Bektas-Cetinkaya & Celik, 2013; Holliday, Hyde, & Kullman, 2004; Sercu, 2006).

The development of language learners' intercultural competence requires language teachers and teacher educators not only to have a well-developed competence themselves, but also to be able to transmit this to their students. It is essential to equip prospective and practicing language teachers with not only the theoretical knowledge but also the ability to apply and disseminate this knowledge. This requires broadening English language teachers' perspectives by raising their awareness of the history and current status of English language, of the role of culture in communication, and of the nature of intercultural competence, and also providing resources which clearly demonstrate how to develop their learners' intercultural competence within the context of teaching English.

English(es)

English has been variously labelled as a Global Language (Crystal, 2003), Global Englishes (Pennycook, 2007), an International Language (Jenkins, 2000; Matsuda, 2012; McKay, 2002), a Lingua Franca (Cogo, 2012; Jenkins, 2007; Seidlehofer, 2001), and World Englishes (Kachru, 1992). English is used worldwide by native and non-native speakers for both intra- and international interactions. Various concepts have emerged to explain the spread of English, such as linguistic imperialism (Philipson, 1992), colonialism (Kachru, 1992), and the economic and military power of Britain and then the USA (Crystal, 2003).

English has been given the status as a world language, not because the number of its native speakers exceeded those of other languages, but rather because it was recognized by almost all countries as a native language, an official language or the primary foreign language taught at school (Crystal, 2003).Corresponding to this three-way categorization, Kachru's sociolinguistic framework explains the functions of English in terms of three concentric circles: inner circle, outer circle and expanding circle.

The inner circle refers to the countries in which English is the dominant language, including UK, USA, Ireland, Canada, Australia and New Zealand. Originally, English emerged from the British Isles, and spread to Ireland. Later it reached America through English settlements, and then Canada through English and American settlements. English reached Australia and New Zealand with the establishment of Britain's "first penal colony in Sydney, thus relieving the pressure on the overcrowded prisons in England. About 130,000 prisoners were transported during the fifty years after the arrival of the first fleet in 1788" (Crystal, 2003, p. 40). After the mid-19th century, they were joined in Australia and New Zealand by a substantial number of free settlers. Although English was the mother tongue in these newly settled countries, different native varieties appeared in each country. These differences occurred at a phonological level, which led to different accents, but also at the lexical and syntactic level; for instance, "biscuit" in British English is "bickie" in Australian English. An American asks "Do you have a car?" while the British equivalent is "Have you got a car?".

The outer circle refers to the former colonies of inner circle countries. In these countries, many acquire English in addition to their mother tongue, which leads to bilingualism or multilingualism. There are more than seventy such countries (Crystal, 2003), including India, Pakistan, Singapore, Hong Kong, Philippines, Ghana, Tanzania, Nigeria, and Malta. English is the official language within these countries, used especially as the language of law and education. This internal use leads to the localization and *nativization* of English (Kachru, 1992), namely, each country developed its own linguistic and pragmatic standards of English, which distinguishes it from the language of inner circle countries. For instance, a British public speaker addresses an audience as "ladies and gentleman", while an African counterpart uses the phrase "sons and daughters of Africa".

The expanding circle refers to the countries which are not the former colonies of inner circle countries, but which teach English as the primary foreign language at school. This circle includes more than 100 countries (Crystal, 2003), such as Turkey, Japan, China, Greece, Poland, Brazil, France, Switzerland, Germany, Italy, Russia, and Egypt. In these countries, English is mainly for international communication, but with a growing intra-national use "for its symbolic effect in such areas as ads, store and brand names and pop culture" (Matsuda, 2012). In expanding circle countries, learners seem to hold the following beliefs: that American and British English varieties are more prestigious than others (Friedrich, 2000), that native-speaker proficiency is the ultimate goal (Matsuda, 2003), and that native English speaker instructors are preferable (Shim, 2002). Language teachers also reflect these attitudes; they prefer native English varieties (Bektas-Cetinkaya, 2016; Sifakis & Sugari, 2005), although they seem to be becoming more aware of English's status as the lingua franca (Bayyurt, 2008).

Culture

Culture can be defined as "a learned set of shared interpretations about beliefs, values, norms, and social practices, which affect the behaviours of a relatively large group of people" (Lustig & Koester, 2006, p. 25). Rather than being born with culture, individuals acquire it through a socialization process within a particular group. It is an abstract phenomenon existing in the mind, and involves beliefs, norms, values and social practices. Despite its intangible nature, culture directly affects our everyday behaviors through beliefs, norms, and values.

When we interact with people from different cultures, we recognize these differences. Some differences are obvious, such as dress and eating habits, but others are more subtle and less visible, and based on the beliefs, norms and values. "Shared beliefs, values, norms, and social practices that are stable over time and that lead to roughly similar behaviors across similar situations are known as cultural patterns" (Lustig & Koester, 2006, p. 85). When we interact, we may not be directly aware of these cultural patterns, but these "shared mental programs" provide the framework for our every thought and action. While some of these cultural patterns are unique to an individual, others are universal. For instance, in any given cultural group, individuals are unique, but all will recognize some shared, universal mental programs, such as the concept of love. In between these unique and universal mental programs, some mental programs/cultural patterns may be exclusive by a particular group. The members of a particular culture or group are not explicitly taught these cultural patterns, but acquire them naturally during their socialization process.

In intercultural interactions, cultural patterns play a crucial role, so it is essential to know what they are, and how they function in communication. Cultural patterns have three components: beliefs, values and norms (Lustig & Koester, 2006). The first component, *beliefs*, are "idea[s]that people assume to be true about the world. Beliefs, therefore, are a set of learned interpretations that form the basis for cultural members to decide what is and what is not logical and correct" (p. 87). The second component, *values*, concern "what a culture regards as good or bad, right or wrong, fair or unfair, just or unjust, beautiful or ugly, clean or dirty, valuable or worthless, appropriate or inappropriate, and kind or cruel" (p. 88). The final component, *norms,* concern behaviors, and are, namely, "the socially shared expectations of appropriate behaviour" (p. 91). The three components, i.e., beliefs, values and norms, differ from culture to culture. American and Turkish culture have a number of differences: American culture values youth, Turkish culture respects elders and entering a house with shoes on is a norm in America, but not in Turkish culture. In a similar vein, the appropriacy of a particular behavior may vary across cultures. For instance, eye-contact in greetings is valued in US culture, but is considered disrespectful in Japanese culture.

Cultural differences, i.e., different beliefs, values and norms, which lead to different behaviors, can cause misunderstandings and communication breakdowns in intercultural encounters. In intercultural communication, aspects of language use are influenced by cultural norms. These culturally-influenced aspects of language are identified as topic, agonism, amplitude-pitch and tone of voice, intonation, turn-taking and indirectness (Tannen, 2006). *Topic* is related to the appropriateness of subjects for conversation. For instance, talking about personal health problems in detail is considered appropriate in Turkish culture but not in German culture. So, if a Turkish person elaborates on health problems at length, a listening German will find the situation very uncomfortable, and although both may speak English, they may find it difficult to find a topic which is equally agreeable to both.

Agonism is related to how to disagree, and to what degree. While in some cultures it is perceived as rude to strongly oppose the ideas of someone you have just met, in others, it is normal. *Amplitude-pitch and tone of voice* is related to voice level, how soft or loud one speaks, and whether the person uses high or low-pitched tones. A loud and assertive voice may be interpreted as enthusiasm and passionate commitment in cultures such as German, but as indicating anger and intimidation in others, for instance, American culture. Similarly, *intonation* is related to music of the language. While speaking English, non-native speakers may use falling intonation in language functions such as making offers, whereas native speakers tend to use rising intonation. As a result, to native speakers, non-native speakers' intended offers may sound more like a statement or even a demand, and risks being perceived as rude.

Another culturally influenced aspect of language is *turn-taking*, which is related to who speaks and when in a conversation. In some cultures, overlapping and interruptions in a conversation is considered to show interest and enthusiasm, but in other cultures, people are expected to listen without interruption. *Indirectness* is about implicitness or explicitness. Each culture may have different conventions regarding the explicitness of sensitive topics. In an intercultural interaction, if one party explicitly states what should be implied according to the interlocutor's cultural norms, that person is perceived as overly blunt.

Cultural biases such as ethnocentrism, stereotyping, prejudice and discrimination have considerable impact in intercultural interactions as well. *Ethnocentrism* can be defined as "the notion that the beliefs, values, norms, and practices of one's own culture are superior to those of others" (Lustig & Koester, 2006, p. 146). Each individual within a given culture considers that their behavior is natural and appropriate, and even universal. Thus, each individual judges others' behavior according to their own cultural framework, and when behavior does not conform to their cultural references, it is considered as wrong, rude, and unacceptable. For instance, in some cultures, dinner starts with salad, and in others, with soup. If you are raised in a culture where a meal starts with soup, you would consider that as natural and universal, and find other cultural practices odd or inappropriate. In intercultural encounters, the concept of a *third place* (Kramsch, 1993) is useful for evaluating practices without bias either towards the framework of the native culture nor the interlocutor's culture.

Stereotypes "are a form of generalization about some group of people. When people stereotype others, they take a category of people and make assertions about the characteristics of all people who belong to that category" (Lustig & Koester, 2006, p. 148). However, in reality there are many differences among people who belong to the same category in terms of gender, nationality, religion, occupation, geographical region, and social class. Although overgeneralizations can sometimes promote mutual understanding, stereotyping treats individuals as a member with every characteristic of their group. Another problem with stereotypes is that these may be based on incorrect overgeneralizations. A person may form stereotypes depending on limited experience with members of that group, or even without any first-hand experience, depending purely on other's ideas or on the media. *Prejudice* "refers to negative attitudes toward other people that are based on faulty and inflexible stereotypes" (p. 151). These negative attitudes may even include hatred of certain groups. The prejudiced tend to overlook evidence that contradicts their views regarding certain groups. The degree may vary, but it appears that all have a degree of prejudice, whether aware of it or not. *Discrimination* is "the behavioural manifestations of that prejudice" (p. 153). Discrimination involves the "unequal treatment of certain individuals solely because of their membership in particular a group" (p. 154). This may even happen in language classrooms.

Intercultural Communicative Competence

Foreign language teaching by nature requires communication, the competence of communication, and communication between culturally different individuals. The concept of "communicative competence" was developed by Hymes to indicate the ability to *use language*. One may have "grammatical competence", but language ability requires more than this. In Europe, van Ek (1986) identified the components of communicative competence as: *linguistic competence, sociolinguistic competence, discourse competence, strategic competence, socio-cultural competence, and social competence.* However, he took the native speaker of that language as a model, and expected language learners to achieve native-speaker competence, an almost impossible goal, generally leading to failure. In foreign language teaching, a more desirable model is a successful bilingual who can use a foreign language to interact successfully with people from various language and cultural backgrounds, through their cultural awareness, an open attitude and intercultural skills.

Byram (1997) proposed the most comprehensive Intercultural Communicative Competence (ICC) model for foreign language teaching, and identified its components as: *linguistic competence, sociolinguistic competence, discourse competence, and intercultural competence.* The innovative part of his model is *intercultural competence*, which consists of *attitudes, knowledge, skills of interpreting and relating, skills of discovery and interaction, and critical cultural awareness.*

The first component of intercultural competence, *attitude*, refers to "curiosity and openness, readiness to suspend disbelief about other cultures and beliefs about one's own" (Byram, 1997, p. 50). The person will be successful in intercultural interaction if

- willing to interact with others and experience their differences in equal terms.
- willing to discover different perspectives and consider issues from both own and others perspectives
- willing to question own cultural practices and values.
- willing to make efforts to adapt to a different culture to varying degrees while experiencing it.
- willing to use conventions of verbal and non-verbal interactions.

The second component of intercultural competence, *knowledge* is the knowledge "of social groups and their products and practices in one's own and in one's interlocutor's country, and of the general processes of societal and individual interaction" (p. 51). The knowledge identified by Byram as necessary for successful interaction is mainly relational, i.e., the knowledge of one's own and one's interlocutor's country, and "how the inhabitants of one country perceive another country" (p. 51). However, since intercultural communications in English occur among non-native speakers of English from a range of cultural backgrounds, it would be an arduous task to teach historical, geographical, social, institutional and relational facts about each and every country of one's potential interlocutors. A more realistic and achievable goal in teaching English would be to provide the basic knowledge of culture and its role in intercultural encounters. One needs to have an understanding of the following: cultural patterns such as value, belief, norms; cultural biases, such as ethnocentrism, stereotyping, prejudice and discrimination; and the culturally-influenced aspects of language, such as topic, agonism, amplitude-pitch and tone of voice, intonation, turn-taking and indirectness. These constitute necessary knowledge for appreciating the complexity of intercultural communication.

The third component of Byram's (1997) intercultural competence is *skills of interpreting and relating*, which refers to the "ability to interpret a document or event from another culture, to explain it and relate it to documents from one's own" (p. 52). Knowledge of the ethnocentric perspective and its acquisition through socialization is a key element in developing this skill. A person who has the skills of interpreting and relating can:

- recognize ethnocentric perspectives
- notice misunderstandings in an interaction
- reconcile conflicting interpretations of a situation

The fourth component of intercultural competence is *skills of discovery and inter-action*, which refers to the "ability to acquire new knowledge of a culture and cultural practices and the ability to operate knowledge, attitudes and skills under the constraints of real-time communication and interaction" (p. 52). A person who has developed the skills of discovery and interaction can:

- Learn the values related to an event or a document from an interlocutor.
- Recognize and seek more information about the important concepts within a culture.
- Notice the similarities and differences in interaction processes, and negotiate their appropriate use.
- use knowledge, attitude and skills appropriately in real-time interactions.

The final component of intercultural competence is *critical cultural awareness*, which refers to "an ability to evaluate critically and on the basis of explicit criteria perspectives, practices and products in one's own and other cultures and countries" (p. 53). This awareness allows the understanding of rationales for judgments of another culture, for instance, labelling certain cultures as uncivilized. A person who has critical cultural awareness can

- interpret implicit and explicit values in a document or an event.
- evaluate a document or an event.
- manage intercultural interactions according to explicit criteria, and, if necessary, adjust criteria used based on knowledge, attitude and skills.

Overview of the Book

The book consists of ten chapters which address various components of intercultural competence in English Language Teaching (ELT). The first chapter presents the Lingua Franca position of the English language, and its pedagogy; the book continues with chapters presenting various means of developing intercultural competence in ELT classrooms; it then addresses the assessment of cultural knowledge, and ends with a discussion of conflict resolution.

While the majority of chapters focus on intercultural competence, the first chapter, "Defining ELF as a Sociolinguistic Concept and a Pedagogical Perspective", focuses specifically on the English language itself, which is defined as an international means of communication among nations and thus, the main tool of intercultural communication. Kemaloglu-Er and Biricik-Deniz give a brief historical view of the English language, examine English as a Lingua Franca within a sociolinguistic framework, and provide pedagogical perspectives with implications for ELF pedagogy.

In Chapter 2, "Culture in English Language Teacher Education Programs: Striving for Intercultural Communicative Competence", Çelik and Erbay Çetinkaya investigate the role of culture and intercultural awareness in teacher education programs. After providing key concepts and models, they examine whether and how intercultural awareness is addressed in language teacher education, and conclude with suggestions for the development of intercultural awareness in teacher education programs. In Chapter 3, "The Representation of Culture into ELT Materials", Özcan and Gürsoy focus on both internationally and locally produced ELT coursebooks as ELT teaching materials, and provide a checklist to evaluate course-books in terms of cultural elements.

The next four chapters focus on developing intercultural competence in the classroom through literature, creative drama, technology and movies, respectively. In Chapter 4, "Developing Intercultural Communicative Competence through Literature", Zorba and Arıkan explore the relationship between literature and culture through literary works, such as John Steinbeck's famous short story "The Chrysanthemums", and provide text examples and associated techniques to assess intercultural competence through literature. "Developing Intercultural Competence through Creative Drama" is the focus of Chapter 5. Güryay aims to increase language learners' emphatic skills through creative drama to develop intercultural competence. She presents an overview of creative drama, the different stages of creative drama, and its specific techniques; then provides comprehensive example creative drama lesson designed to develop intercultural competence. Chapter 6 "Raising Intercultural Awareness through Technology" by Yangın-Ekşi and Aşık explores historical background and current implementations of technology use for cultural awareness, such as social media use, online games, podcasting, computer-mediate communication and telecollaboration. The chapter provides language teachers with guidelines, sample tasks and best practices for exploiting technology for intercultural awareness. In Chapter 7, "Developing Intercultural Competence through Movies" Nickolson and Arıkan focus on facilitating global literacy through the use of cross-cultural films in English language classrooms. They explore the cultural concepts of ethnocentrism, discrimination, stereotypes and acculturation through three films with intercultural themes.

In Chapter 8, "Raising Intercultural Awareness of Young Learners", Yangın-Ersanlı and Akman-Yeşilel describe the characteristics and learning processes of young learners before presenting a lesson plan designed to raise young learners' cultural awareness. Assessment is the focus of Chapter 9, "Classroom Assessment of L2 Cultural Knowledge". Börkan introduces and exemplifies various assessment techniques and approaches for the assessment of intercultural communicative competence. In the final chapter of the book, "Conflict Resolution in Intercultural

Communications", Kacmaz explores the nature of conflict, different conceptions of conflict, the conflict resolution process, and the communication skills needed. He also provides some implications of conflict resolution for language learning.

References

Atay, D. (2005). Reflections on the cultural dimension of language teaching. *Language and Intercultural Communication*, 5, 222–236.

Bayyurt, Y. (2008). *A lingua franca or an international language: The status of English in Turkey*. ELF Forum, Helsinki: Finland.

Bektas-Cetinkaya, Y. (2014). Extension of teacher knowledge: Developing the intercultural competence of pre-service foreign language teachers in Turkey. *Novitas ROYAL*, 8(2), 153–168.

Bektas-Cetinkaya, Y. (2016). English as a lingua franca: Awareness and attitude of prospective teachers in Turkey. *International Journal of TESOL and Learning*, 5(1&2), 1–16.

Bektas-Cetinkaya, Y. & Börkan, B. (2012). Intercultural communicative competence of preservice language teachers in Turkey. In Y. Bayyurt & Y. Bektas-Cetinkaya (Eds.), *Research Perspectives on Teaching and Learning English in Turkey* (pp. 107–119). Frankfurt am Main: Peter Lang.

Bektas-Cetinkaya, Y. & Celik, S. (2013). Perception of Turkish EFL teacher candidates on their level of intercultural competence. In H. Arslan & G. Rata (Eds.), *Multilingual Education: From Theory to Practice* (pp. 345–362). Newcastle upon Tyne: Cambridge Scholars Press.

Byram, M. (1997). *Teaching and Assessing Intercultural Communicative Competence*. Clevedon: Multilingual Matters.

Byram, M., Gribkova, B. & Starkey, H. (2002). *Developing the Intercultural Dimension in Language Teaching*. Strasbourg: Council of Europe.

Cogo, A. (2012). English as a lingua franca: Concepts, use and implications. *ELT Journal*, 66(1), 97–105.

Council of Europe. (2001). *Common European Framework of Reference for Languages: Learning, Teaching, Assessment*. Strasbourg: Council of Europe.

Crystal, D. (2003). *English as a Global Language*. Cambridge: Cambridge University Press.

Friedrich, P. (2000). English in Brazil: Functions and attitudes. *World Englishes*, 19, 215–223.

Furstenberg, G. (2010). Making culture the core of the language class: Can it be done? *The Modern Language Journal*, 94(2), 329–332.

Holliday, A. R., Hyde, M. & Kullman, J. (2004). *Intercultural Communication*. London: Routledge.

Jenkins, J. (2000). *The Phonology of English as an International Language.* Oxford: Oxford University Press.

Jenkins, J. (2007). *English as a Lingua Franca: Attitude and Identity.* Oxford: Oxford University Press.

Jenkins, J., Cogo, A. & Dewey, M. (2011). Review of developments in research into English as a Lingua Franca. *Language Teaching*, 44(3), 281–315.

Kachru, B. B. (1992). *The Other Tongue: English across Culture.* Illinois: University of Illinois Press.

Kramsch, C. (1993). *Context and Culture in Language Teaching.* Oxford: Oxford University Press.

Lustig, M. W. & Koester, J. (2006). *Intercultural Competence.* Boston: Pearson.

Matsuda, A. (2003). The ownership of English in Japanese secondary schools. *World Englishes*, 22(4), 483–496.

Matsuda, A. (Ed.) (2012). *Principles and Practices of Teaching English as an International Language.* Bristol, UK: Multilingual Matters.

McKay, S. L. (2002). *Teaching English as an International Language.* Oxford: Oxford University Press.

Pennycook, A. (2007). *Global Englishes and Transcultural Flows.* London: Routledge.

Philipson, R. (1992). *Linguistic Imperialism.* Oxford: Oxford University Press.

Seidlehofer, B. (2001). Closing a conceptual gap: The case for a description of English as a lingua franca. *International Journal of Applied Linguistics*, 11(2), 133–158.

Seidlhofer, B. (2011). *Understanding English as a Lingua Franca.* Oxford: Oxford University Press.

Sercu, L. (2006). The foreign language and intercultural competence teacher: The acquisition of a new professional identity. *Intercultural Education*, 17, 55–72.

Shim, R. J. (2002). Changing attitudes toward teaching English as a world language in Korea. *Journal of Asian Pacific Communication*, 12(1), 143–158.

Sifakis, N. C. & Sugari, A. M. (2005). Pronunciation issues and EIL pedagogy in the periphery: A survey of Greek state school teachers' beliefs. *TESOL Quarterly*, 39(3), 467–488.

Tannen, D. (2006). Language and culture. In R. W. Fasold & J. Connor-Linton (Eds.), *Language and Linguistics* (pp. 343–372). Cambridge: Cambridge University Press.

Elif Kemaloglu-Er and Esma Biricik Deniz

1 Defining ELF as a Sociolinguistic Concept and a Pedagogical Perspective

Introduction

English as a lingua franca (ELF) used as the common means of communication among speakers from diverse cultural and linguistic backgrounds in every nook and corner of today's global world is a dynamic social reality experienced every second on our planet by millions and millions of non-native speakers. In these interactions typically taking place in multilingual and multicultural settings, ELF is continuously appropriated by the individual interlocutors as a means of communication to reach mutual intelligibility. ELF, therefore, with its variability-rich nature, cannot be defined with the norms of Standard English established by native speakers. It is a complex phenomenon with a life of its own marked with linguistic, pragmatic and cultural flexibility and shaped by the contextualized experiences of the interlocutors with myriad practices, constructs, and performances.

English has achieved this lingua franca status because of a tremendous growth in the number of second language speakers of English in the world today who believe it is to their benefit to acquire English as an additional language. From a time in the 1960s when the majority of speakers were thought to be first language speakers, we moved into a situation where non-native speakers far outnumbered native speakers of English and dynamically communicate in not only face-to-face communications but also digital platforms. This global power of English has given rise to many studies on the spread and status of English around the world, the new varieties of English and the use of English as a lingua franca, which altogether paved the way for questioning and challenging the dominance and supreme authority of native speakers over English. The idea that the only owners of English are native speakers has been shattered by the efforts to define English as a lingua franca and set a comprehensible framework for ELF, a highly complex construct, in both sociolinguistic and pedagogical terms.

In this chapter we are going to define ELF as not only a sociolinguistic concept but also a pedagogical perspective and elaborate on the relevant meanings and implications. ELF as a term presents a great potential of conceptualizations as the use of English language today is interwoven into various contextualized practices, constructs, and performances. In this sophisticated context of ELF use, it is our objective to make what ELF means clear to the reader and explore the meanings of several related phenomena.

ELF as a Sociolinguistic Concept

For some, an international language may be associated with the number of its native speakers; however, a language cannot function as a language of wider communication unless it is spoken by a great number of speakers of other languages (McKay, 2002). As Crystal (2003) clarifies a language reaches a genuinely global status when it gains a special role that is recognized in every country across the world either in the form of an official language used in such domains as government, courts, media and education or a priority in foreign language education. One chief reason why a language becomes global is the power of its people – "especially their political and military power" (Crystal, 2003, p. 9). English has been no exception as very well documented (e.g. Crystal, 2003, 2008; Graddol, 1997, 2006). The expansion of British colonial power which reached its peak towards the end of nineteenth century and the emergence of the United States as the leading economic power of the twentieth century are two factors which have mainly contributed to the present-day world status of English (Crystal, 2003). Braj Kachru (1985) has suggested we think of the spread of English around the world as three concentric circles representing the ways in which the language has been acquired and is currently used. The *inner circle* represents the traditional bases of English, where it is the native language: Included in this circle are the USA, the UK, Ireland, Canada, New Zealand, and Australia. The *outer circle* or *extended circle* includes countries where English is not the primary language but it has become a part of a nation's institutions as an official language. It is also important for historical reasons and plays a crucial role as a "second language". The circle includes India, Nigeria, the Philippines, Bangladesh, Pakistan, Malaysia, Kenya, Singapore, and over fifty other territories. The *expanding circle* or *extending circle* involves those nations where English plays no historical role of colonization or is given no special governmental status but where its importance is recognized well as an international language and is widely used as a foreign language. This circle includes China, Japan, Turkey, Greece, Poland, Russia, and much of the rest of the other nations in the world population.

In recent years, various terms which are used interchangeably have emerged as a way of referring to the current status of English and the global spread of it all around the world such as *World English(es), International English, Global English(es)*. The uses of English internationally include speakers of English as a native language (Kachru's inner circle), speakers of English as a foreign language (Kachru's expanding circle) and the speakers of indigenized and nativized varieties (Kachru's outer circle). Seidlhofer (2003) indicates wherever English is used for cross-cultural communication, it can be referred to as *English as an international language (EIL)*. There are other terms that can be used for EIL such as *English as a lingua franca* (Gnutzmann, 2000), *English as a global language* (Crystal, 2003), *English as a world language* (Mair, 2003). What these terms have in common is that they all signal a difference from the default conception of the language; namely, the norms employed by its native speakers (Seidlhofer, 2003). Thus, the uses of English internationally may take place in conditions that are different from the ones in which the language is only associated with its native speakers and its place of origin. Jenkins (2006) mentions the so-called phenomenon of *World Standard English* which refers to a hypothetical and monolithic form of English. This standard form based on American or British norms represents a monocentric view rather than a pluricentric one (Jenkins, 2006).

The term "lingua franca" has been susceptible to many different interpretations and explanations. As Jenkins (2015) suggests, the diversity of ELF is rapidly increasing due to more and more people engaging in intercultural communication using English as a means of communication. This means that theorizing ELF cannot also be fixed or stabilized, but that ELF researchers and scholars need to update their conceptualizations of the phenomenon in accordance with new empirical research findings.

In its purest form, ELF can be defined as "the world's most extensive contemporary use of English, in essence, English when it is used as a contact language between people from different first languages (including native speakers)" (Jenkins, 2014, p. 2). In her study, Seidlhofer (2004, p. 214) presents a conceptualization of ELF as a phenomenon questioning the deference to hegemonic native speaker norms in all contexts and emphasizing the legitimacy of variation in different communities of use. In their study, Jenkins, Cogo and Dewey (2011) suggest that ELF is a paradigm according to which most speakers of English are non-native speakers and all English varieties both native and non-native are accepted in their own right rather than evaluated against a native speaker benchmark. ELF, then, has taken on a life of its own, free to a significant degree from the norms established by its native speakers (Seidlhofer, 2004).

In her study, Jenkins (2015) presents a three-phase discussion of ELF research. The first phase when World Englishes was a new field of enquiry comprises the early World Englishes literature, e.g. Kachru (1985, 1991, 1992), Smith (1981). The research of this phase focused on form; primarily on pronunciation and lexicogrammar. It is during this phase that Jenkins (2000) proposed the "Lingua

Franca Core" consisting of few native segmental and prosodic items which are crucial for protecting the quality of intelligibility. She focuses on phonological features since her studies reveal that pronunciation is the most common cause of intelligibility problems in ELF interactions. She has termed the "Lingua France Core" (LFC), which is based on the empirical data drawn from ELF interactions. LFC evaluates which phonological features are and which are not vital for intelligible pronunciation in lingua franca contexts. The ones that cause intelligibility problems are included in the LFC whereas the ones that do not are excluded from the LFC and considered to be "non-core". In order for intelligibility Jenkins (2000) suggests focusing on nuclear stress and specific core sounds including most consonants sounds, and the distinction between long and short vowels. She also emphasizes the importance of articulatory setting which is related to the physical factors in the articulation of sounds such as the shape of the tongue or the lip and cheek posture. Jenkins's LFC does not include –th sounds and the dark l allophone which are proved not to be vital for mutual intelligibility in the conversations, that's why they are non-core. This approach to pronunciation takes native speaker model not as a goal but as a kind of reference to keep non-native varieties from moving too far apart from each other (McKay, 2002).

It was again in this phase that Jenkin's proposals were followed by Seidlhofer's (2004) Vienna-Oxford International Corpus of English in which she presented a set of lexicogrammatical items that are regularly used by speakers from different first language backgrounds without causing loss of intelligibility. As Jenkins (2015) points out, during the early 2000s, ELF researchers believed in the possibility of describing and even codifying ELF varieties in order to legitimize ELF use. In the following phase, the problem of focusing on only the form was identified and there was a shift from the traditional variety-oriented ELF to variability as a defining characteristic of ELF communication. In this phase, ELF researchers were in agreement that it is a "fallacy" to think that in the outer and expanding circle countries, the goal of learning English is to interact with native speakers. As Jenkins (2015) points out, the conceptual evolution of ELF will never stop as long as the phenomenon exists and new empirical evidence about the nature of it constantly emerges. That's why; she highlights the need for further conceptualizations and retheorizations comprising the third phase of ELF research. This phase focuses on the multilingual nature of ELF communication. Jenkins (2015) mentions a "multilingual turn" in applied linguistics which argues against native speaker "competence" and in favor of "multicompetent users" (Cook, 2002). This has led to regard language as social practice and multilingualism as a resource rather than an obstacle. ELF is now characterized not only by its variability but also its complexity, fluidity and emergent nature (Jenkins, 2015).

The phenomenon of ELF challenges established interpretations of the term "native speaker" and its implicational exclusivity of ownership. Rajadurai (2007, p. 93) lists three myths about native varieties:

Myth 1: The native variety should constitute the norm.
Myth 2: The native speaker is always the best judge of what is intelligible.
Myth 3: The native speaker is always the best representative of what is intelligible.

As Rajadurai (2007) summarizes, first, the native variety is seldom in non-native contexts, so imposing the native variety as the norm is unreasonable since the lingua franca use of English means that diversity is to be expected. Second, most interactions in English today occur in the absence of a native speaker, therefore there is no reason to assume that a native speaker's judgment plays the biggest role in determining the intelligibility of non-native varieties. Finally, an inner circle speaker may not always be the most intelligible one and as Rajagopalan (2004) also suggests, being a monolingual, the native speaker may sometimes even be handicapped in performing communicative tasks in World Englishes.

Within ELF, *intelligibility* is of primary concern. However, it is a complex matter and what is meant by *intelligibility* needs to be considered carefully in ELF research. While discussing the issue of intelligibility, McKay (2002, p. 52) makes distinction between the terms "intelligibility" – recognizing an expression; "comprehensibility" – knowing the meaning of the expression; and "interpretability" – knowing what the expression signifies in a particular sociocultural context. As McKay (2002) suggests, for instance, if the interlocutor recognizes that the word 'salt' is an English word but not Spanish, then it is intelligible to her. If she knows the meaning of the word, then it is comprehensible to her and if she understands that there is a request for salt in the phrase "Do you have any salt?", then she interprets the language. Despite these distinctions, the term, intelligibility is often used in general sense covering all these three meanings (McKay, 2002). There are research studies (Jenkins, 2000; Seidlhofer, 2004) showing the importance of intelligibility in different aspects of language such as phonology, pragmatics and lexico-grammar and they present norms different from those of native speakers.

Jenkins (2006) associates SLA researchers' difficulty with ELF with their inability to distinguish a lingua franca from a foreign language. For most ELF researchers, however, ELF and EFL (English as a Foreign Language) are two entirely different phenomena. In her study, Jenkins (2006) presents the differences between ELF and EFL in detail. These differences are also summarized by

Jenkins, Cogo and Dewey (2011). First of all, ELF is part of the Global Englishes paradigm which highlights the irrelevance of the deference to a native speaker benchmark to evaluate the native and non-native varieties of English. However, EFL is part of the Modern Foreign Languages paradigm whose ultimate goal is to be able to communicate effectively with native speakers who are the target interlocutors of that language and to gain near-native competence. That is, in EFL paradigm, most interaction involving non-native speakers is with native speakers of the language, and non-native speakers' goal is to approximate the native variety as closely as possible. Second, ELF sees non-native Englishes as different rather than deficient whereas in EFL perspective, the differences between native and non-native Englishes are considered as errors and deficiencies that are associated with incomplete L2 acquisition. Thus, from an ELF perspective, non-native speakers are no longer failed native speakers of EFL but highly competent communicators who can rely on their multilingual resources that monolingual native speakers lack. As Jenkins (2006) points out the linguistic outcome of ELF and EFL may be the same but these forms which do not cause communication problems are labelled "variants" in ELF and "errors" in EFL.

So far, we have explored the sociolinguistic dimensions of the ELF notion but one must know that ELF is not only a multifarious sociolinguistic concept, but also a pedagogical perspective, the features of which are described in the next section.

ELF as a Pedagogical Perspective

On the basis of the reality of variability and functionality in ELF use deviating from native norms, ELF can be taken as an accepting and flexible way to understand English language teaching. Accordingly, ELF is a perspective which acknowledges the non-native varieties of English in their own right and the non-native users of language with their own unique characteristics (i.e. with their own use of English, L1s and sociolingual and sociocultural backgrounds) (Jenkins, Cogo, & Dewey, 2011). According to this perspective, deviations from the native norms are not signs of incompetence if they do not deteriorate intelligibility: They are acceptable variations specific to non-native speakers to attain their communicative goals. This perspective also accepts non-native speakers with their own features (e.g. their variations, L1/s, local cultures and their own sociolinguistic and sociocultural paths) and argues that these features should be integrated in English lessons. ELF perspective contrasts with the mainstream EFL perspective dominating English classes, according to which non-native speakers' goal is to approximate the native variety as closely as possible and deviations from native norms are accepted to be signs of incompetence. Also, EFL perspective in its typical form puts emphasis on native speakers' cultures and neglects cultural backgrounds and intercultural insights of non-native speakers. Hence, in very simple terms EFL as a pedagogical perspective highlights Standard English and its culture – usually British or American – whereas ELF as a pedagogical perspective highlights non-native varieties and non-native speakers' own local cultures. Bayyurt & Sifakis' (2013) following itemization about the main aspects of ELF as a pedagogical perspective may also act as a helpful guide for practitioners willing to apply this form of pedagogy:

> (i) ELF is seen as primarily spoken (oral) orientation, (ii) the teacher engages in a manner of teaching that does not focus primarily on correction but on intelligibility, (iii) the teacher designs/ adapts tasks that do not demand that learners lose their own personality and cultural background to the effect of blindly imitating native speaker behavior, (iv) the teacher allows for learners using elements (linguistic, cultural or otherwise) from their L1/mother tongue or even other languages they may share, (v) the teacher adopts a pedagogy that advocates active planning for and attention to learners' differences in classrooms.

If we are to adopt an ELF perspective in English language teaching (ELT), Seidlhofer (2011) suggests, first we must acknowledge that most users in the world are non-native speakers, and a great number of them are indeed communicatively capable because it is witnessed that language partially and imperfectly learnt according to the conventional point of view can be put into implementation in communicative use. That is, learners judged to "fail" according to native norms can be or become effective users of English. When these states of affairs are taken into consideration, two options arise and either one can lead to a teaching competence, learners rarely attain and may not require as subsequent users of language. On the other hand, it is also possible to set realistic and attainable objectives which fit the needs of the actual users of the language. The first option is to go on with a pedagogy based on purely native norms with the assumption that all uses of English in the world should be compatible with native norms and somehow an approach to teaching will be devised in order to have the learners acquire it. However, records show that a majority of learners who put what is learnt into ELF use are stigmatized as incompetent users of the language and thought to be stuck somewhere in the interlanguage. The second approach would be to accept the reality that native speaker competence is not an achievable goal and what is learnt does not and cannot match up with what is taught. Thus, the goal should be the development of a capability for effective use which involves exploiting whatever linguistic resources are available no matter how formally defective they are.

Unlike the pedagogical approach that emphasizes native speaker competence and sees partial acquisition as deficient, according to the one suggested by Seidlhofer (2011), all language acquisition is partial and can never be otherwise. Nobody can know a language, nothing but the language. So, the notions of both learning a language and native speaker competence are fictions. Thus, how much language learners acquire is irrelevant. What matters is the extent to which whatever parts they have learnt can serve to activate their capability for using and thus for extending their linguistic source. As for forms to be used, Seidlhofer (2011) states it would be pointless to prescribe a set of ELF norms as a set of ENL (English as a Native Language) norms detached from their function. What is really significant is that the language should engage learners' reality and activate the learning process. Any kind of language taught aiming for this effect is appropriate and this will be a matter of local decision. This is what Kumaravadivelu (2004) suggests with his post-method pedagogy where teachers are advised to rely on their context-sensitive local knowledge to identify problems and apply solutions. So, what is crucial is not what language is presented as input but what learners make out of it and how they do this. The pedagogic significance of ELF pedagogy is that it shifts the focus of attention to the learner and the learning process. As a result, what matters is not the language content, but how it is exploited for learning so what teaching materials offer is not that significant but the important thing is how they are used. Jenkins (2007) similarly states that "it would be unreasonable to expect tests or materials to focus for production of ELF forms" (p. 244).

MacKenzie (2014) also refers to the fact that it is now premature to present a model for ELF pedagogy where ENL forms are absent and it is standard variety that should act as a linguistic model both in the context of EFL and ELF. On the other hand, Dewey (2012) points out that teachers should spend relatively less time on ENL forms, especially those not widely used in other varieties and should not penalize non-native-led innovative forms which are intelligible. This "post-normative approach" suggested by Dewey (2012) is not against a Standard English model. It highlights being selective about the norms to be included in the classroom through reflective thinking, which would then shed light on the uniqueness of each learner.

Also exposing learners to a broad range of accents right from the start through listening and speaking activities is a useful approach in ELF pedagogy to raise learners' awareness of English varieties (Kohn, 2015; MacKenzie, 2014; Matsuda, 2009). According to Matsuda (2009), instead of depending exclusively on audios that accompany the textbook, one can supplement it with textual and audio samples of other varieties of English. Also inviting international visitors and residents in the community to the class is another useful method. Such interaction not only creates opportunities for students to interact in English but also shows them that being an effective user of English does not require being a native speaker. Seidlhofer (2004) even suggests teaching language awareness as a separate course which would include instruction on ELF awareness as one element. In addition to this, as mentioned by various scholars above, language teachers must devote time and energy to communication activities and attract attention to common cooperative, interactive, pragmatic or discourse strategies like focusing on intelligibility rather than correctness, requesting repetition or clarification when necessary, signaling non-comprehension in a face-saving way, making things explicit, paraphrasing utterances by adjusting their form, and making prompts and suggestions.

Furthermore, in the ELF classroom, L1 is a reality of plurilingualism and it is something that both learners and teachers can make use of when necessary. Thus abandoning the traditional language teaching practice of banning L1 is necessary. As stated by Cook (2002), the English classroom is potentially a code-switching setting where all members speak at least two languages. Alptekin (2002) underlines the importance of the learner's first language and cultural background in becoming interculturally and communicatively competent users of English. Akbari (2008) also points out that L1 is an asset that can facilitate teaching and communication in the L2 class. On the other hand, L1 should not be used as the language of instruction, yet it has useful functions like maintaining discipline in the classroom, providing instructions for certain activities and/or explaining delicate points of grammar or abstract vocabulary.

Another remarkable point to be taken into consideration in ELF pedagogy is the inclusion of learners' local culture. As Holliday (2009) states native speaker models of English must withdraw from defining the nature of culture and language, to allow local educators and students to claim English and English language education in their own terms. Bayyurt (2006) maintains local culture can well become a part of the English classroom together with the international culture. This requires instructors' knowledge and experience about both culture types and/or collaboration of native and non-native teachers with their balanced cultural shares in the educational setting. Ho (2009) suggests activities leading learners to compare, contrast and reflect on native speakers' and nonnative speakers' cultures. Akbari (2008) views the same issue through the angle of critical pedagogy and he proposes relating the classroom context to the wider social context with the aim of social transformation through education. Akbari (2008) emphasizes basing one's teaching on students' local culture in L2 learning is mainly due to two facts: (1) non-native speakers of English have a distinct cultural identity of their own and in most communicative settings people would try to communicate their own cultural values, not those of the target culture; (2) inclusion of local culture in class enables learners to critically think about different facets of the culture they live in and suggest and apply solutions and changes in the society where they are needed. Matsumoto (2011) contends local culture is not restricted to traditional culture, such as "kimono" in the case of Japan, or knowledge of the formal political system, history, and the constitution. Any beliefs and practices in which students' experience is situated (e.g., school, family, community) also constitute the local culture. To illustrate, interacting with international visitors and trying to answer their questions require the knowledge and the ability to explain such beliefs and practices. Creating an English website of their own school or hometown for international visitors is another possibility. These experiences allow students to critically reflect upon what they take for granted and work on skills to elaborate on their local culture while practicing their English in authentic global communicative situations.

Integration of ELF into English classes can be achieved in explicit and implicit ways as defined by Kemaloglu-Er and Bayyurt (2018, 2019a, 2019b). In explicit ELF integration learners are directly informed about the meaning and importance of ELF while in implicit ELF integration, the teacher makes no direct reference to the notion of ELF. Explicit ways can be practiced by overt and direct means like lectures, readings and videos, through which learners are informed about ELF and related concepts including the global status of English, the status and roles of native speakers and non-native speakers, non-native varieties in English use, and the importance of mutual intelligibility. Moreover, learners are prompted to ponder on the issues and make their own discoveries of ELF by critical reflections, reflective interactions and real-life experience. On the other hand, in implicit ELF integration, ELF is incorporated into lessons covertly and indirectly without any explicit explanations about ELF. In the lessons with implicit ELF integration there are ELF-related elements tacitly included in the lessons such as (i) video displays of non-native speakers' speaking English with different varieties, (ii) non-native speakers' and learners' own cultures, (iii) intelligible variations deviating from standard norms not corrected by the teacher, (iv) limited use of learners' L1 in the classroom. An originality of implicit ELF integration is that in real-life practice, it derived from the creative efforts of the teachers eager to implement ELF pedagogy, but were unable to do so explicitly because of the pressure of Standard English-bound education contexts emphasizing native speaker superiority. Thus, implicit forms of practice may provide safe space for teachers. According to Kemaloglu-Er and Bayyurt (2019a), in practicing an ELF-oriented syllabus, it is necessary that explicit/implicit phenomenon should be viewed not as a binary notion, but a continuum and even a "repertoire" of sensible combinations. Thus, teachers can start practicing ELF integration in an explicit or implicit way, but it is recommended that these two practices complement each other in the flow of their own syllabus to effectively raise learners' ELF-awareness.

The data collected from pre-service teachers exposed to an ELF-aware teacher education course have revealed creative ways of ELF incorporation into the English classroom (Kemaloglu-Er, 2017a). As for a sample task of ELF integration, the teacher starts the lesson displaying learners sample videos of speakers from the Inner, Outer and Expanding Circles speaking English with their own varieties. S/he then uses these videos as means to introduce them to the concepts of ELF and mutual intelligibility as well as Kachru's circles. After introducing the learners to the relevant concepts through lectures and whole class interactions, the teacher divides the class into groups and asks them to analyze a NNS-NNS conversation video with regard to variations which do not deteriorate intelligibility and what they feel about them. After the groups report their own findings and attitudes about the interaction, the teacher emphasizes the fact that NNSs display variability in terms of English use and in their interactions and they may use English deviating from native norms, but as long as these deviations do not deteriorate intelligibility, they would not cause communication problems. S/he adds that having variations is in the very nature of NNS reality, which must be acknowledged in its own right rather than assessed against the NS benchmark according to the ELF paradigm and according to this paradigm, with variability and complexity of English use and with differing sociolinguistic and sociocultural backgrounds, each NNS is unique and each interaction involving NNSs would present original cases not abiding by native norms. After these explanations to the classroom, the teacher can assign the class the following portfolio homework aiming for ELF-focused interaction and critical reflection for the whole term: "Each learner is supposed to find an e-friend from another country; the e-friend should be a NNS as well. Then, they are supposed to interact with each other, both through written language (e.g. using Facebook) and spoken language (e.g. through Skype). Then, everyone has to record their experiences and prepare a portfolio to submit at the end of the year. Moreover, every week, an hour will be dedicated to this process, the learners will share their experiences, including the difficulties they have had during communications, how they have got over those problems and achieved mutual intelligibility and what they think about the process as NNSs".

As shown by this sample ELF-oriented task, in order to integrate ELF in the classroom, there needs to be a context-sensitive methodology initiated in accordance with the dynamics of the bilingual classroom. As stated by Alptekin (2010) bilinguals are neither the sum of two monolinguals (Grosjean, 1992, 1995) nor the representatives of the sum of two cultures. They display a special configuration, blending aspects of the two languages and two cultures. From the perspective of ELF, their development presents a unique form of multicompetence comprising a synthesis of a variety of cultural aspects that interact with bilingualism. Thus, what Alptekin (2010) suggests is an eclectic ELT methodology underlain by the notion of a multicompetent bilingual whose distinct state of mind reflects the interactive effects of two or more languages and cultures.

Bayyurt (2012) also highlights the importance of a socially sensitive pedagogy for English language learning and mentions that the widest use of English in the world is for communication among non-native speakers in diverse cultural contexts, thus any pedagogy not taking this fact into account will fail to meet the needs of learners. According to Jenkins (2007), ELF researchers share the need for a pluricentric rather than a monocentric approach to teaching and use of English. Finally, according to Bayyurt and Akcan (2015) for the development of an ELF pedagogy, it is feasible to start with teacher education, which in turn would influence the design of language teaching materials and the criteria used for assessing achievement in language learning. The ELF-aware teacher education model devised by Bayyurt and Sifakis (2015a, 2015b) is one prominent sample for such education and it aims to make the teachers tangibly and critically aware of the ELF perspective through intense theoretical training, active teaching practice, continuous critical reflection as well as reflective interactions with colleagues. Such models can raise the ELF-awareness of not only teachers but also their students. Thus, teacher education is a vital component in raising ELF-awareness in a society. There are several ways to raise the ELF awareness of pre-service teachers as suggested by Biricik Deniz (2017), Biricik Deniz, Ozkan and Bayyurt (2016, 2019) Kemaloglu-Er (2017a, 2017b), Kemaloglu-Er and Bayyurt (2018, 2019a, 2019b). To illustrate, prospective teachers can be exposed to intense ELF-related theoretical training and perform reading, critical reflection and in-class and online discussion tasks with their colleagues on the meaning and implications of ELF as a sociolinguistic concept and a pedagogical paradigm. They can also analyze different NNS-NNS interactions and accents by using online sources and explore specific dynamics of communication between NNSs such as variations which do not deteriorate intelligibility and/or communication strategies and discuss them with their colleagues. Another task would be their recording their own conversations with other NNSs and/or NSs and analyze the recordings with regard to intelligible variations deviating from native norms. As for ELF pedagogy, together with their supervisors, mentor teachers and colleagues, they can also attempt to devise their own ELF-aware lesson plans and/or projects, apply them in the form of peer teaching and/or practicum, and reflect on these ELF-focused practices via both self-assessment and collective evaluations.

ELF awareness should be a crucial component of teacher education since teachers are the active agents of change and social enlightenment about the NNS reality can well start in the English classroom. However transformative education is a collaborative process. Only with the fruitful collaboration of stakeholders in ELT including teachers, teacher educators, academics, curriculum designers, materials and test writers, school administrators, parents and most importantly learners can we effectively raise ELF-awareness and implement ELF-aware pedagogy in the English classroom.

Conclusion

The pivotal status of English assures that this global language structures the interactions in cultural, sociopolitical, academic, educational, diplomatic, technological, financial and many more issues around the world. Deference to native norms seems to be irrelevant for the sociolinguistic reality of all these contexts where English is used. The emergence of such a social reality also promotes the legitimacy of variation in the use of English. ELF is a paradigm which implies that most speakers of English are non-native speakers and all English varieties both native and non-native should be acknowledged in their own right rather than evaluated against a native speaker benchmark. ELF, then, can be said to be a unique entity independent to a certain extent from the norms established by its native speakers. Becoming such a complexity, ELF has triggered numerous controversies about various issues including the status of both native and non-native speakers, questioning the attachment to Standard English and native speaker norms, the importance of intelligibility in interactions, the ownership of English and the intercultural competence.

When ELF is taken as a pedagogical perspective, it can be defined as an approach which acknowledges the non-native speaker reality in and out of the English classroom in its own right, is tolerant to deviations from the norms of Standard English as long as they are intelligible and views non-native speakers' own features (e.g. their English variations, L1/s, local cultures and their own sociolinguistic and sociocultural backgrounds) as an inseparable part of ELT and argues that these features should be incorporated into English lessons. This integration may be achieved in explicit and/or implicit ways and in a feasible

ELF-aware syllabus, the recommendation is the accompaniment of explicit and implicit ELF integration.

Bilinguals are not the sum of two monolinguals and representatives of the sum of two cultures in Grosjean's (1992) and Alptekin's (2010) terms as they display a *sui generis* configuration where two or more languages and cultures interact with each other. ELF as a pedagogical perspective highlights the exclusive nature of these interactions and promotes the language learning experience of non-native speakers by avoiding strict adherence to native norms. In order that ELF can be integrated effectively into English lessons, teacher education is necessary since teachers in collaboration with learners are the guiding forces of all pedagogical practices.

It is therefore essential to raise the ELF-awareness of pre- and in-service English language teachers with novel teacher education models, which would possibly affect and change the native speaker-oriented and Standard English-bound pedagogical mentalities and implementations. The world of ELT is in need of paradigms and practices embracing both native and non-native speakers with their own varieties and identities.

References

Akbari, R. (2008). Transforming lives: Introducing critical pedagogy into ELT classrooms. *ELT Journal, 62*(3), 276–283.

Alptekin, C. (2002). Towards intercultural communicative competence in ELT. *ELT Journal, 56*(1), 57–64.

Alptekin, C. (2010). Redefining multicompetence for bilingualism and ELF. *International Journal of Applied Linguistics, 20*(1), 95–110.

Bayyurt, Y. (2006). Non-native English language teachers' perspective on culture in English as a foreign language classrooms. *Teacher Development, 10*(2), 233–247.

Bayyurt, Y. (2012). Proposing a model for English language education in the Turkish socio-cultural context. In Y. Bayyurt & Y. Bektaş-Çetinkaya (Eds.), *Research perspectives on teaching and learning English in Turkey: Policies and practices* (pp. 301–312). Frankfurt: Peter Lang.

Bayyurt, Y., & Akcan, S. (2015). Current perspectives on pedagogy for ELF. In Y. Bayyurt & S. Akcan (Eds.), *Current perspectives on pedagogy for English as a lingua franca* (pp. 1–9). Berlin: Mouton de Gruyter.

Bayyurt, Y., & Sifakis, N. C. (2013). Transforming into an ELF-aware teacher. Paper presented at Verona University New Frontiers in English Language Teaching Symposium, Verona, Italy.

Bayyurt, Y., & Sifakis, N. C. (2015a). Developing an ELF-aware pedagogy: Insights from a self-education programme. In P. Vettorel (Ed.), *New frontiers in teaching and learning English* (pp. 55–76). Newcastle upon Tyne: Cambridge Scholars Publishing.

Bayyurt, Y., & Sifakis, N. C. (2015b). ELF-aware in-service teacher education: A transformative perspective. In H. Bowles & A. Cogo (Eds.), *International perspectives on teaching English as a lingua franca* (pp. 117–135). Basingstoke: Palgrave Macmillan.

Biricik Deniz, E. (2017). A case study on ELF-aware pre-service language teacher education model: Theory into practice (Unpublished doctoral dissertation). Cukurova University, Adana, Turkey.

Biricik Deniz, E., Ozkan Y., & Bayyurt, Y. (2016). English as a lingua franca: Reflections on ELF-related issues by pre-service English language teachers in Turkey. *The Reading Matrix, 16*, 144–161.

Biricik Deniz, E., Özkan, Y., & Bayyurt, Y. (2019). ELF-awareness in pre-service English language teacher education: A case study from Turkey. *Hacettepe University Journal of Education*. Advance online publication. doi: 10.16986/HUJE.2019055867

Cook, V. (2002). Background to the L2 user. In V. Cook (Ed.), *Portraits of the L2 user* (pp. 1–28). Clevedon: Multilingual Matters.

Crystal, D. (2003). *English as a global language.* Cambridge: Cambridge University Press.

Crystal, D. (2008). Two thousand million. *English Today, 24*(1), 3–6.

Dewey, M. (2012). Towards a post-normative approach: Learning the pedagogy of ELF. *Journal of English as a Lingua Franca, 1*(1), 141–170.

Gnutzmann, C. (2000). Lingua franca. In M. Byram (Ed.), *The Routledge encyclopedia of language teaching and learning* (pp. 356–359). London: Routledge.

Graddol, D. (1997). *The future of English? A guide to forecasting the popularity of the English language in the 21st century.* London: British Council.

Graddol, D. (2006). *English next.* London: British Council.

Grosjean, F. (1992). Another view of bilingualism. In R. J. Harris (Ed.), *Cognitive processing in bilinguals* (pp. 51–62). Amsterdam: Elsevier Science.

Grosjean, F. (1996). Living with two languages and two cultures. In I. Parasnis (Ed.), *Cultural and language diversity and the deaf experience* (pp. 20–38). Cambridge: Cambridge University Press.

Ho, S. T. K. (2009). Addressing culture in EFL classrooms: The challenge of shifting from a traditional to an intercultural stance. *Electronic Journal of Foreign Language Teaching, 6*(1), 63–76.

Holliday, A. (2009). The denial of ideology in perceptions of 'nonnative speaker' teachers. *TESOL Quarterly, 43*(4), 669–689.

Jenkins, J. (2000). *The phonology of English as an international language.* Oxford: Oxford University Press.

Jenkins, J. (2006). Current perspectives on teaching World Englishes and English as a lingua franca. *TESOL Quarterly, 40*(1), 157–181.

Jenkins, J. (2007). *English as a lingua franca: Attitude and identity.* Oxford: Oxford University Press.

Jenkins, J. (2014). *English as a lingua franca in the international university: The politics of academic English language policy.* Oxon: Routledge.

Jenkins, J. (2015). Repositioning English and multilingualism in English as a lingua franca. *Englishes in Practice, 2*(3), 49–85.

Jenkins, J., Cogo, A., & Dewey, M. (2011). Review of developments in research into English as a lingua franca. *Language Teaching, 44*(3), 281–315.

Kachru, B. (1985). Standards, codification and sociolinguistic realism: The English language in the outer circle. In R. Quirk & H. G. Widdowson (Eds.), *English in the world: Teaching and learning the language and literatures* (pp. 11–30). Cambridge: Cambridge University Press.

Kachru, B. (1991). World Englishes and applied linguistics. *ERIC, ED 347 805,* 178–205.

Kachru, B. (1992). World Englishes: Approaches, issues and resources. *Language Teaching, 25,* 1–14.

Kemaloglu-Er, E. (2017a). Integrating ELF-awareness into pre-service teacher education: Insights from theory and practical experience (Unpublished doctoral dissertation). Boğaziçi University, Istanbul, Turkey.

Kemaloglu-Er, E. (2017b). Design, implementation and evaluation of ELF-aware lesson plans—Lessons, activities and tasks for EIL teacher preparation. In A. Matsuda (Ed.), *Preparing teachers to teach English as an international language* (pp. 221–223). Bristol, UK: Multilingual Matters.

Kemaloglu-Er, E., & Bayyurt, Y. (2016). ELF-aware teacher education with pre-service teachers: A transformative and technology enhanced case from Turkey. In N. Tsantila, J. Mandalios, & M. Ilkos (Eds.), *ELF: Pedagogical and interdisciplinary perspectives* (pp. 261–267). Athens: Deree.

Kemaloglu-Er, E., & Bayyurt, Y. (2018). ELF-aware pre-service teacher education: Teaching practices and reflections from Turkey. In L. Cavalheiro

(Ed.), *Preparing English language teachers for today's globalized world* (pp. 47–63). Lisbon: Húmus.

Kemaloglu-Er, E., & Bayyurt, Y. (2019a). ELF-awareness in teaching and teacher education: Explicit and implicit ways of integrating ELF into the English language classroom. In N. C. Sifakis & N. Tsantila (Eds.), *English as a Lingua Franca for EFL contexts* (pp. 147–163). Bristol, UK: Multilingual Matters.

Kemaloglu-Er, E., & Bayyurt, Y. (2019b). Project-based and ELF-aware pre-service teacher education in Turkey: Sample cases of discovery, creativity, interaction and multicultural diversity. In A. Gras-Velazquez (Ed.), *Project-based learning in second language acquisition: Building communities of practice in higher education* (pp. 82–97). London: Routledge.

Kohn, K. (2015). A pedagogical space for English as a lingua franca in the English classroom. In Y. Bayyurt & S. Akcan (Eds.), *Current perspectives on pedagogy for English as a lingua franca* (pp. 51–67). Berlin: De Gruyter Mouton.

Kumaravadivelu, B. (2004). Critical language pedagogy: A postmethod perspective on English language teaching. *World Englishes, 22*(4), 539–550.

MacKenzie, I. (2014). *English as a lingua franca: Theorizing and teaching English*. London: Routledge.

Mair, C. (Ed.). (2003). *The politics of English as a World Language*. Amsterdam: Rodopi.

Matsuda, A. (2009). Globalization and English language teaching: Opportunities and challenges in Japan. *The Language Teacher, 33*(7), 11–14.

McKay, S. L. (2002). *Teaching English as an international language: Rethinking goals and approaches*. Oxford: Oxford University Press.

Rajadurai, J. (2007). Revisiting the concentric circles: Conceptual and sociolinguistic considerations. *The Asian EFL Journal, 7*(4), 111–130.

Rajagopalan, K. (2004). The concept of "World English" and its implications for ELT. *ELT Journal, 58*(2), 111–117.

Seidlhofer, B. (2003). *A concept of international English and related issues: From 'real English' to 'realistic English'?*. Language Policy division, Council of Europe, Strasbourg.

Seidlhofer, B. (2004). Research perspectives on teaching English as a lingua franca. *Annual Review of Applied Linguistics, 24*, 209–239.

Seidlhofer, B. (2011). *Understanding English as a lingua franca*. Oxford: Oxford University Press.

Smith, L. E. (Ed.) (1981). *English for cross-cultural communication*. London: Macmillan.

Servet Çelik and Şakire Erbay Çetinkaya

2 Culture in English Language Teacher Education Programs: Striving for Intercultural Communicative Competence

Introduction

Addressing culture and cultural diversity in education has become a major area of concern in recent decades, and public education systems worldwide have taken measures to promote multiculturalism, intercultural awareness, and other diversity-related competencies. With an eye to promoting a more socially conscious, just, and inclusive global community, as well as mitigating the historical marginalization of minority populations, diversity has been pinpointed as one of the most critical issues in modern education. As such, the European Union, along with many of its partner states, has expressed an increasingly positive stance toward addressing the issues of multilingualism, multiculturalism, and numerous other diversity-related concerns in the public education process (Tongal, 2015). Despite the rhetoric, however, this enthusiasm does not always translate into policy, and in countries such as Turkey, few specific objectives have been set in this regard (Tarman, 2010; Tongal, 2015).

However, one branch of the Turkish education system that has taken proactive measures to address diversity, at least in terms of culture and intercultural awareness, is the field of English language education; and the national English language curricula for elementary and secondary students consider intercultural competence as a key component and descriptor of language proficiency, and contain explicit recommendations for incorporating culture in language learning (Çelik, 2013, 2014a, 2014b; Çelik & Gül Peker, 2019; Çelik & Karaca, 2014). Accordingly, there is an expectation that culture-related topics and issues will be handled in the course of English language instruction. As such, the responsibility for addressing culture ultimately falls to classroom teachers of English as a foreign language (EFL). However, as Bektaş-Çetinkaya and Çelik (2013) and Yazıcı, Başol, and Toprak (2009) point out, few in-service EFL teachers in Turkey, much less English language teaching candidates, believe that they are equipped with sufficient intercultural skills of their own, and they have little confidence in their ability to convey these skills to learners. Furthermore, culture-related content in the teaching materials approved by the Turkish Ministry of National Education

(MoNE) is often found to be inadequate (Çelik & Erbay, 2013), leaving teachers with little support in this regard. This situation raises the question of whether Turkey's English language teaching programs are doing enough to provide EFL teacher candidates with both the intercultural awareness and the diversity-related pedagogical skills they need to address these issues effectively in their future practice.

This chapter, therefore, is an attempt to uncover whether diversity through culture and intercultural awareness is addressed in English language teacher education in Turkey. The chapter will start off by clarifying the related terminology and concepts such as culture, intercultural awareness, and intercultural competence, drawing from the work of prominent names in the field. It will then summarize a well-known model of Intercultural Communicative Competence (ICC), as its suggested dimensions will be referenced throughout the chapter. The reader will afterward be briefly informed of the current state of language teacher education in Turkey with respect to the issue in question. This will be followed by an examination of whether diversity-related goals relating to cultural awareness are communicated in language teacher education programs, as well as in practice, in the Turkish context. The chapter will conclude with various strategies from diverse educational and cultural backgrounds as potential ways to address these issues in language teacher education in Turkey. It is anticipated that the information provided in this chapter may ignite an enthusiasm in teacher educators to prepare EFL teachers for their role in dealing with cultural diversity and inclusion, as well as in classroom teachers to question the many inequalities they face on a daily basis, both in and out of the school setting.

Important Terms

For a full grasp of the issues discussed throughout this chapter, clarification of some important terms may be useful. With this in mind, some of the most commonly used terminology is defined here to serve as a reference point.

Culture

This dynamic term has been characterized in a number of ways. Some have described it as an iceberg (Peterson, 2004; Weaver, 1986), with a small portion visible above the surface of the water, while the vast bulk is hidden from view; or as an onion (Hofstede, 1991), with multiple layers; or as a fish swimming in water (Brislin, 2000), immersed in the element around it. For the purposes of this chapter, however, we turn to the definition of Peterson (2004), as "the relatively stable set of inner values and beliefs generally held by groups of people in countries or regions and the noticeable impact those values and beliefs have on the people's outward behaviors and environment" (p. 17).

Intercultural Awareness

It has long been understood that awareness of one's own culture, as well as the cultures of other societies and the similarities and differences between them, is crucial to successful cross-cultural interactions. This skill is referred to as intercultural awareness and has been defined as the "ability to communicate and collaborate effectively with people whose attitudes, values, knowledge and skills may be significantly different from [one's] own" (Cushner, 2007, p. 27).

Intercultural Competence

Intercultural interactions help build bridges across cultural boundaries and advance "effective and appropriate behavior and communication in intercultural situations" (Deardorff, 2011; p. 66). Wintergerst and McVeigh (2011), therefore, refer to intercultural (or cross-cultural) awareness as an understanding of "how people from different cultures communicate among themselves and with others, as well as how people perceive their own culture and the world around them" (p. vii).

Intercultural Sensitivity

This term is concerned with the affective dimension of intercultural awareness and should be understood as the promotion of a willingness to approach, recognize and value cultural differences when communicating with people from diverse backgrounds.

Intercultural Communicative Competence (ICC)

Building on the concepts defined above, Byram (1997) goes beyond and describes intercultural communicative competence as individuals' "ability to interact in their own language with people from another country and culture, drawing upon their knowledge about intercultural communication, their attitudes of interest in otherness, and their skills in interpreting, relating and discovering" (p. 70). In this regard, interculturally competent individuals are flexible and open-minded people who are interested in and cognizant of cultural differences, who tend to fight against stereotypes, who modify their behaviors for the sake of effective communication, and who feel motivated and show willingness to collaborate with people from different linguistic and cultural backgrounds to solve global problems (Cushner & Chang, 2015).

Byram's Model for Addressing Intercultural Competence in Language Education

Interest in developing intercultural competence in various fields has led the way to numerous models of intercultural (communicative) competence. Spitzberg and Changnon (2009), for example, mention more than twenty models targeting specific contexts and disciplines, ranging from education to healthcare, sales to management. However, for the purpose of this chapter, the model that stands out in the field of foreign language education will be referenced: Byram's (1997) *Model of Intercultural Communicative Competence (ICC)*.

Byram's model identifies five interrelated components of intercultural communication: *attitudes; knowledge; skills of interpreting and relating; skills of discovery and interaction;* and *critical cultural awareness.* In this regard, *attitudes* refer to the views we hold concerning the cultural differences we come across during our encounters with others. Byram argues that the type of attitudes that are needed for successful interactions are objectivity, impartiality, openness and curiosity towards detecting the meanings embedded in others' expressions and behaviors. It is important to note that any deviation in attitudes (positive or negative) from neutrality correlates to biases that could impair our understanding of the intentions of others.

The second component of his model deals with the *knowledge* individuals have regarding other countries or social groups and that of their own—including any stereotypes they might harbor about their culture or that of others in interacting with people from diverse backgrounds. Knowledge here also includes the processes of interaction at an individual and societal level. This signifies declarative knowledge about how social identities are acquired and how they shape people's worldviews, as well as procedural knowledge of how to act in specific circumstances.

Another component Byram delineates is *skills of interpreting and relating*, embodying the ability to analyze and decode a document or an event from another culture and to describe it in relation to the documents and events in one's own culture. The next refers to *skills of discovery and interaction*, denoting the ability to expand the existing repertoire of cultural knowledge and practices and to engage and put to the test the attitudes, knowledge and skills in actual interactions. The difference between the last two components lies in the fact that the former draws from the existing knowledge, and that interpretation can take place beyond the limits of real-time communication.

As Byram (1997) argues, these four components of the model "can in principle be acquired through experience and reflection, without the intervention of teachers and educational institutions" (p. 33). This can take place simply by living and through informal learning opportunities that come in many forms. In this respect, the fifth and final dimension of Byram's model, *critical cultural awareness*, differs from the others. Critical cultural awareness refers to the ability to evaluate the perspectives, practices, and products of both local and diverse cultures based on precise criteria, and to develop, through an exchange of stereotypes in interacting with others, a critical lens on one's own and others cultures. This awareness requires experiencing all four previous levels and is placed at the center of the schema around all other components, emphasizing the role of foreign language education and teaching.

Overall, Byram considers that foreign language teaching in the context of formal education is key for building critical cultural awareness. Thus, he suggests that language instructors should ground the teaching and assessment of these five components within the communicative goals in their planning in order to develop these skills in their students. This practical educational aspect of his model is important in distinguishing intercultural competence (the five components outlined in the model) and intercultural communicative competence (intercultural competence combined with foreign language learners' use of language and communicative competence – linguistic, sociolinguistics, discourse, strategic, sociocultural and social competences) in various learning settings and modes, such as the classroom, fieldwork and independent learning.

As a setting designed to address language and communication, Byram sees the foreign language classroom as offering ample potential for teaching intercultural communicative competence. Language reflects and embodies culture, and therefore, it is natural for cultural elements to be addressed in foreign language learning. Therefore, the question that the teachers face should not be whether, but how culture should be approached and taught in the context of language learning.

The System of English Language Teacher Education (ELTE) in Turkey: Initial and In-service Teacher Education

Teacher Education Programs in Turkey's Public Universities

In Turkey, the training of English language teachers is most commonly carried out within a four-year university program. Responsibility for language teacher training thus falls primarily to the centralized Council of Higher Education (CoHE), which maintains control of the nation's public universities and oversees all aspects of their educational programs. Once teacher candidates have completed their education and been appointed to a classroom position, the MoNE, which is responsible for the public schooling process at the elementary and secondary levels, provides support for teachers' professional development (Öztürk & Aydın, 2019).

Before acceptance to a university teacher education program, candidates sit for a nationwide university entrance exam designed and implemented by the Student Selection and Placement Centre. English language teacher candidates also take the English Language Proficiency Test, which includes 80 multiple-choice questions on reading comprehension, grammar, and vocabulary. Because Turkey's English as a Foreign Language (EFL) curriculum at the high school level often focuses on preparing students for standardized tests, other language skills such as speaking, listening, and ICC are often neglected. As a result, teacher candidates often enter their university programs with a low level of English proficiency; thus, the first year of initial ELTE is devoted to enhancing their language-related skills. At the same time, they take two courses on pedagogical terms and educational sciences; one course designed to develop their awareness and skills in information technologies; an additional foreign language class; and two general culture courses on Turkish language and Turkish history. In the second year, pre-service teachers take subject-matter courses on linguistics, literature, and teaching methodology, in addition to general education courses. The third year of the four-year program focuses primarily on methodology courses relating to the teaching of English to diverse students, including young learners. In this year, teacher candidates also take courses in lesson planning and preparation of instructional materials. Finally, in both semesters of their fourth year of study, teacher candidates participate in a teaching practicum course, during which they observe real classrooms and teach demo-lessons under the guidance of their university supervisor and a mentor teacher at their practicum school (Aydın, 2016; Öztürk & Aydın, 2019).

Alternative Training for English Language Teacher Candidates

Aside from the four-year English language teacher education programs, a second path to becoming an EFL teacher is available through a pedagogical formation certificate program. This training program is offered for students who have graduated with degrees in English Language and Literature, Translation and Interpreting, Linguistics, or American Culture and Literature, but who plan to become English teachers. The one-year program offers some background coursework in educational sciences, as well as subject-matter knowledge; however, the program is often criticized as insufficient for preparing candidates with the necessary teaching skills in such a short period of time (Aydın, 2016; CoHE, 2014; Yüksel, 2012).

Certification and Appointment to a Teaching Position

Once teacher candidates have completed their initial training, they are required to sit for a nationwide exam entitled Public Personnel Selection Examination (KPSS). This exam consists of multiple-choice questions covering four major areas, including social sciences, pedagogical knowledge, subject-matter knowledge and language proficiency. In addition, teacher candidates who achieve an adequate ranking on the exam are subjected to a 10-minute oral interview by officers of the MoNE. In this process, they are asked some general questions about education, psychology and technology. Their total score from the exams and oral interview determines the state school where they are to be assigned as an English language teacher (CoHE, 2014; Yüksel, 2012). Approximately half of the program graduates do not score high enough on the exams to be appointed to a teaching position (Öztürk & Aydın, 2019).

In-Service Teacher Training

Once a candidate has been assigned as a classroom teacher, in theory, the first year of teaching is intended as an internship year, with a lower pay rate, reduced class sizes, and observation by a mentor teacher. However, in practice, with already oversized classes and a general shortage of teachers, most novice teachers are placed directly into regular classrooms and essentially find themselves in a "learn-on-the-job" scenario (Tarman, 2010). From this point, the professional development of in-service teachers falls primarily to the MoNE, which provides various teacher education opportunities. For instance, at both at the beginning and the end of each school year, teachers are offered two-week seminars on a number of topics related to subject-matter knowledge and life skills training (Öztürk & Aydın, 2019). These usually one-shot events with no follow-ups are criticized for being ineffective on a number of grounds, and they are not viewed as meeting the actual needs and demands of language teachers (Çelik, 2016). Some of the shortcomings mentioned in the literature are their heavy focus on theory, rather than practice; poorly-qualified trainers; a top-down structure; organizational issues with scheduling; and teachers' resistance and reluctance to play a part in these activities (Çelik, 2016; Öztürk & Aydın, 2019; Uysal, 2012;

Uztosun, 2018). The absence of systematic and effective in-service supervision, support and quality management for teachers ultimately means that they are left to find their own way in the teaching profession.

Given these concerns, the MoNE has recently set forth an initiative published in a document titled *Teacher Strategy Paper 2017–2023* (MoNE, 2017) to address issues regarding initial teacher training and professional development of teachers. One of the three major objectives of the Teacher Strategy Paper is to "ensure continuous personal and professional development of teachers" (p. 2). The document furthermore lists goals such as "establishing a periodic performance evaluation system to identify teachers' professional development needs" and "increasing the quality of activities that target teachers' personal and professional development, starting from teachers' candidacy training" (p. 2). However, there are concerns as to the likelihood of materialization of these plans (Öztürk & Aydın, 2019), and thus, it is still too early to determine whether these actions will help improve the quality of in-service training for English language teachers.

Challenges in Addressing Intercultural Awareness in the EFL Classroom

With the structure of English language teacher education outlined in the previous sections, we now turn to the ongoing efforts to address cultural diversity with respect to EFL teachers and teaching. In this regard, both the definition and the main goals of schooling have undergone drastic changes worldwide over the past few decades. As Cushner and Mahon (2009) point out, building effective relationships with others to resolve global issues, beyond a mere understanding of such issues, is now the driving force that dictates global competitiveness in interconnected societies in the age of information. Thus, public education systems can no longer limit themselves to implementing local goals, and educators cannot continue to teach with the interest only in populations and issues that directly surround them. However, while this reality is generally accepted, schools continue to struggle with socializing students to their role as world citizens and with successfully equipping them with the values, attitude, skills and knowledge needed to function well in various groups and contexts (Cushner & Mahon, 2009).

As Cushner (2011) observes, both pre- and in-service teachers are often ethnocentric themselves, living in isolated homogenous groups; thus, they may fail to see or may simply ignore the cultural differences of other groups. Often, they are predisposed in their ways of thinking and acting, and therefore quick to judge and even discriminate against others on the basis of cultural disputes and misunderstandings. In most cases, it is not that they oppose the idea of interculturalism or the notion of intercultural competence, but rather that they do not possess the *sine qua non* to make changes to their pedagogical practices. Consequently, it is not realistic to assume that they can somehow develop their students' intercultural competence when their own approach to culture is partial and distorted in many ways.

On the other hand, in Turkey, as in many other parts of the world, English language education is regarded as one of the subject areas that should be taking measures to address cultural diversity. Theoretically, this should be carried out in the language classroom through teachers' efforts to expose students to culture-related topics and issues, increase their awareness of diversity, and equip them with the necessary skills to communicate successfully in a variety of intercultural settings. As such, fostering the critical intercultural competence of language teachers in terms of linguistic and cultural diversity is a vital concern "in the era of globalization, transnationalism, and multilingual/ multiculturalism" (Shin & Jeon, 2018, p. 125) In other words, teacher educators have a responsibility to raise "internationally-minded" (Cushner, 2007, p. 27) or "globally competent teachers" (Cushner, 2011, p. 601). Because developing intercultural competence is a lifelong process, rather than a one-off experience, it should be integrated into teacher education as an ongoing aspect of both initial teacher training and in-service professional development programs (Chang, 2018).

Yet, while both pre- and in-service EFL teachers have expressed awareness of the importance of culture for teaching English in Turkey, in their practice, it has been widely observed that linguistic objectives continue to be emphasized more than cultural outcomes, as in other countries around the world (Önalan, 2005; Pena-Dix, 2018; Salazar & Agüero, 2016). This may result in part from the fact that cultural objectives in the institutional syllabus for elementary and secondary EFL teaching are limited, and they are not formally evaluated (Kahraman, 2016). Thus, while Turkish teachers typically assert that they make an effort to integrate culture into their classes, they do not see it as their primary concern, nor do they consider it as a separate objective. Any integration they do carry out is generally limited to concrete and observable elements (e.g., foods, clothing, and holidays), as such surface-level components are practical and easy to teach. Furthermore, teachers tend to use only the instructional materials provided to them by the MoNE, which contain minimal references to culture; they do not make a conscious effort to provide any supplementary materials to increase their students' cultural awareness and competence. This reticence may result from the overloaded curriculum, lack of time, teach-to-the-test pressure, lack of (inter)cultural experience, and finally, absence of culture-specific courses in their teacher education programs that foster familiarity with foreign cultures (Kahraman, 2016).

The Need to Address Intercultural Competence in English Language Teacher Education

The urgency to develop and nurture the desired skills in teachers to deal with steadily increasing cultural diversity raises the issue that Turkey's English language teaching programs are not doing enough to provide EFL teacher candidates with both the intercultural awareness and the diversity-related pedagogical skills they need to address these issues effectively in their future practice. In fact, the core English language teacher education curriculum specified by the Council of Higher Education and outlined in earlier in this chapter has long included only limited standards and content designed to prepare future teachers for dealing with pluralism in their teaching (CoHE, 2014; Karakaş, 2012). Until a recent revision of the CoHE's undergraduate teacher education program for English Language Teaching (ELT), which was implemented in 2018, the program components, expectations and outcomes were left, for the most part, to the discretion of individual departments and universities. Under these circumstances, it was unclear if, and how, the ELT programs were responding to the need for cultural diversity—whether they included any culture-related courses; which culture or diversity-related skills, goals or outcomes were being addressed in these courses; and how many EFL teacher candidates were actually enrolling in and taking advantage of them.

To illuminate this issue, Çelik (2017) undertook a systematic survey of the elective courses offered in the ELT programs of Turkish universities to illustrate the level of awareness demonstrated by those programs of the need to prepare future teachers of English to address cultural diversity in their practice, and to highlight their efforts (or lack thereof) to do so; and to call attention to the necessity of incorporating culture and intercultural awareness in a more comprehensive and uniform manner in Turkey's foreign language teacher education programs. For those institutions that did provide online information concerning their course offerings (38 in all), the programs were examined through content analysis, and courses related to cultural diversity were identified and indexed using course titles and descriptions. For the purposes of the study, cultural diversity was evaluated in terms of a focus on foreign cultures, multiculturalism, intercultural skills, pragmatics, and so on. Other diversity-related concerns, such as gender and inclusive instruction for special needs, while important, were not considered within the scope of the investigation. According to the results, among the thirty-eight ELT programs surveyed, only eighteen culture-related elective courses were identified, distributed between fourteen different universities (representing approximately 38 % of the programs). Accordingly, Çelik (2017) argued that although the MoNE's EFL curricula included specific provisions for the teaching of culture at the elementary and high school levels, it could be seen from data that Turkey's English Language Teaching programs fell far short in terms of preparing future teachers of English with the skills needed to support intercultural awareness in their students. As such, it was no surprise that Turkish EFL teachers and teacher candidates do not feel that they possess the necessary skills to deal with culture in the classroom, as noted by Bektaş-Çetinkaya and Çelik (2013) and Yazıcı, Başol, and Toprak (2009). With this in mind, Çelik (2017) concluded that it was necessary to draw the attention of ELT department heads to this shortcoming and to encourage them to include culture-related courses as electives in their four-year degree programs.

Reform of English Language Teacher Education to Address Intercultural Awareness

In light of these concerns, the CoHE (2018) has recently introduced revisions to the standardized teacher education curriculum that was introduced earlier in the chapter. The courses in the new program are organized under three categories: Pedagogical knowledge (PK), content knowledge (CK) and general knowledge (GC). Teacher candidates are required to complete 155 course hours (148 credits/240 ECTS credits) to graduate; forty-eight percent of these courses comprise CK, while 34 percent cover PK and the remaining 18 percent address GK. One major improvement in the new program is the increase in the number of elective courses. Starting with the third semester of study, teacher candidates must complete sixteen electives in the above-mentioned three categories (6 CK, 6 PK, and 4 GK courses).

An analysis of the new ELTE program (based on the set course content determined by the CoHE) reveals some required and elective courses that might be of use in preparing teacher candidates for dealing with cultural diversity in their future classes. For instance, core courses such as *Foreign Language 1* and *2, English Literature 1* and *2,* and *Literature in Language Teaching 1 and 2* may be said to directly contribute to the goals that are primarily associated with intercultural competence. It should be noted, however, that several other required courses, while they do not directly focus on culture and cultural diversity, include cultural elements and outcomes that may address the cultural knowledge, attitudes and skills required for intercultural communicative competence. Just to name a few, discussion of cultural foundations of education in *Introduction to Education (PK)*; the relationship between culture and education in *Sociology of Education (PK)*; cultural revolutions in *Atatürk's Principles and History of Turkish Revolutions 2 (PK)*; cultural perspectives of teaching of English in *Approaches to Learning and Teaching English (CK)*; and the appropriateness of cultural content in *Course Content Development in English Language Teaching* (CK) may all, in theory, lead to important culture-related goals.

Elective courses, on the other hand, deserve more attention here, as any changes in the content of the core courses were comparatively modest. In this regard, the addition of dozens of elective courses, making up 25 percent of the program, may be upheld as one of the key aspects of the improvements. For instance, PK courses such as *Educational Anthropology, Inclusive Education, Character and Values Education, Comparative Education*, and *Individualizing and Adapting Instruction*; GK courses such as *Human Rights and Democracy Education, Human Relations and Communication*, and *Culture and Language*; and CK courses such as *Language and Society, World Englishes and Culture; Pragmatics and Language*, and *Sociolinguistics and Language Teaching* are valuable additions to the program and key to developing teacher candidates' intercultural communicative competence. As such, it would be helpful to briefly mention the content of each here.

To start with the PK courses, *Educational Anthropology* is culture-loaded in that it aims at clarifying culture-related terms such as acculturation, adaptation, and sub-culture, to list but a few. In this sense, it is beneficial in terms of increasing pre-service teachers' awareness of cultural differentiation; school cultures and ethnographies; cultural backgrounds and functions of education; popular culture; globalization; cultural interaction; parent and child roles in Turkish families; and so on. Next, *Inclusive Education* covers factors such as culture that distinguish learners from each other and how these factors could be integrated in effective communication; as well as instructional decisions that teachers make regarding course planning, methods and approaches, classroom discourse, course texts and materials, and classroom tasks and activities; in order to ensure quality education for all. Another culture-related elective PK course is *Character and Values Education,* which handles, among other things, issues such as values crisis and education in modern and multicultural societies; the role of values education in cultural development; and examples of values education from the history of Turkish education and culture. As the next PK course that contributes to cultural competence, *Comparative Education* aims to guide teacher candidates to compare and contrast education systems of different countries regarding various aspects, such as structure, functioning, human resources and reforms. The final culture-related PK course is *Individualizing and Adapting Instruction*, which covers issues such as individualization of education; ways of differentiating, personalizing, and individualizing instruction; adaptation of educational practices; and examples of considerations to promote and support the needs and learning of individual students.

Fewer GK elective courses are offered than PK electives. Among these, *Human Rights and Democracy Education* aims at increasing teacher candidates' awareness of democratic education and maintaining an appropriate classroom atmosphere at all educational levels. *Human Relations and Communication*, furthermore, seeks to highlight the role of intercultural differences in human relations. The one other culture-related GK course available is titled *Culture and Language*. This course is rich in content, incorporating a wide range of information and discussions such as basic concepts of language and culture; sources and elements of culture; oral and written culture; material and spiritual culture; culture from an individual and a societal perspective; culture as a binder or a divider; acculturation, cultural diffusion and adaptation; culture in terms of cognitive, symbolic, structural-functional approaches; the relationship between culture, language, cognition and reality; the role of language as a conveyor of information and culture; development and transfer of language and culture; national identity and language; dynamics of changes in culture and language; national cultures; and globalization, multilingualism and multiculturalism.

The new program also introduces a few CK courses with predominantly cultural outcomes. To illustrate, *Language and Society* deals with issues such as the relationship between language and society; geographical and social differences; social layers; and changes in language. *World Englishes and Culture*, on the other hand, aims at increasing teacher candidates' awareness of English diversity around the world and the role of culture in instruction and teaching materials. Another CK course, *Pragmatics and Language*, sets out to show how to apply the term "politeness" to language education, as well as instructing students on how to design materials to present vocabulary in context. Lastly, *Sociolinguistics and Language Teaching* informs teacher candidates about changes in language use across regions and social groups, with an overall goal of showing them how language changes in society and how this should be linked to foreign language teaching.

Aside from the elective courses that address culture-related issues more directly, there are also electives that contribute to the development of intercultural competence in an indirect manner or through secondary cultural outcomes. *Critical and Analytical Thinking (PK)*, for instance, can be considered instrumental in accomplishing the unbiased perspective Byram (1997) emphasizes with respect to the dimension of *attitude* in ICC.

In view of the discussion above, the program updates concerning the introduction of numerous culture-related courses might appear to be significant in terms of preparing teachers for cultural diversity. However, three points should be kept in mind in terms of their results. First, there is no guarantee that individual programs will actually adopt these potentially useful courses and offer them in their course rosters. Second, it is debatable, even when offered, that all teacher candidates will in fact take and benefit from them, as they may hypothetically choose other courses. Finally, we have no way of ensuring the quality (including their own intercultural competence) of individual instructors of these courses, leading to questions about the possibility of reaching the expected outcomes and consistent results for all teacher candidates within and among Turkey's ELT programs.

Accordingly, foreign language teacher educators should acknowledge that offering courses that directly addresses intercultural communicative competence may not be a complete solution for enabling teacher candidates to acquire what this concept demands. Thus, the teaching of ICC should not be limited to specific courses. Rather, the acquisition of ICC should be seen as a complex and ongoing process requiring teachers in all aspects of education to provide students with not only the mere knowledge of others, but the opportunities for training, experience and self-reflection. This is the case in both "teacher educator to teacher candidate" interactions in a language teacher education program and "teacher to student" contact in a foreign language classroom. Thus, ICC goals should be spread over all courses (especially CK courses) in language education programs as a means to provide teacher educators more flexibility to handle the attitudes, knowledge and skills in the context communicative goals and competences, and to use different language skills as milieus for teaching ICC.

What Can Language Teacher Education Programs Do?

Some specific steps and procedures may be implemented by faculty in language teacher education programs to teach ICC; these will be discussed in following section. Çelik and Kasap (2019), for instance, suggest that the elective courses on culture could be made mandatory. While this requires further updates by the CoHE and might not be feasible for some time, individual ELT programs can take measures to secure this in practice. This, of course, would not come without criticism. On the other hand, the related literature documents some additional ways to prepare teacher candidates by providing authentic learning

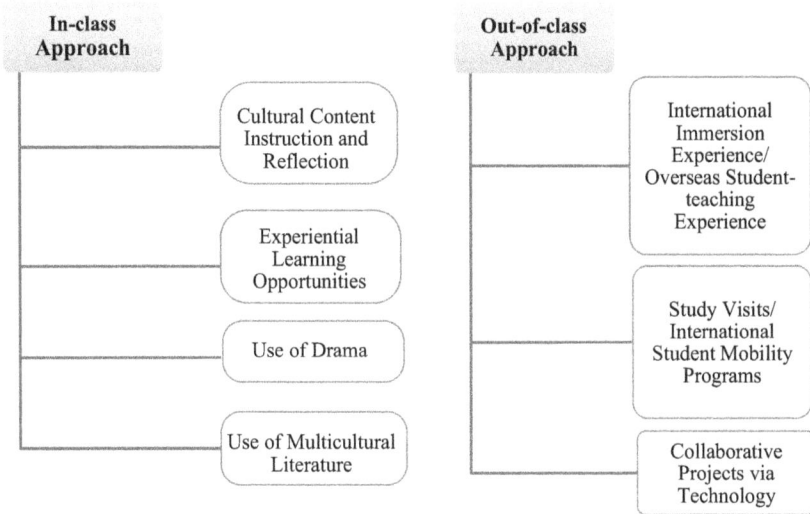

Fig. 1: Approaches to Facilitate Diversity via Cultural Awareness

opportunities that reflect the globalized 21st century in which they will eventually teach. These may be divided into two main categories as in-class and out-of-class approaches, as illustrated in Fig. 1.

The In-Class Approach to Intercultural Awareness

Through the teacher education process, teacher candidates may be provided with tasks and activities that will help them to internalize the concept of diversity and address it in their classrooms. *Receiving cultural content instruction,* as indicated in Fig. 1, is one way to enhance cultural awareness and intercultural competence when pre-service teachers do not have ample opportunities to travel or live abroad. In this sense, teacher educators can introduce basic culture-related concepts through avenues such as pop culture and authentic reading materials, which can support awareness of the existence of others (Shin & Jeon, 2018). In addition, they may assign intercultural tasks such as analyzing cultural values in instructional materials, examining miscommunication in intercultural conversations, and identifying stereotypical images and ethnocentric perspectives in teaching texts. They might also ask them to analyze books and watch films to identify such misunderstandings and stereotypes. Through these activities, they have the opportunity to develop intercultural skills in that they learn to identify miscommunications and overcome them for more successful interactions.

From another perspective, teacher candidates may be encouraged to *critically reflect* on their own beliefs and views. In this process, pre-service teachers may go beyond superficial cultural knowledge through defining cultural concepts, noticing culture in intercultural interactions, learning about other cultures and comparing and contrasting them with their home culture. Through critical self-reflection, students, pre-service and in-service teachers may become more sensitized to the backgrounds, values, thoughts, and cultures of other people, leading to open-minded attitudes towards diversity and acceptance of others different from them. They may also feel more willing to research different cultures. Through this undertaking, they are supported in becoming successful leaders who care about their students, as well as their families, developing "professionalism, flexibility and intentionality" (Thapa, 2020, p. 166) in this regard.

Aside from addressing their own intercultural competence, pre-service teachers should also be familiarized with methods for teaching others about culture. These include, for example, using literary texts of various genres, such as poetry, short stories, and novels; utilizing arts such as visual arts, films, and music; introducing cultural stimuli such as posters, paintings, realia, maps, and so on to the classroom; exploring cultural festivals, holidays, and traditions; encouraging students to conduct research for deeper knowledge about diverse cultures and present their finding in the classroom; applying kinesthetic learning activities such as role-plays, drama, and simulations; involving students in experiential learning and giving contact tasks in their society; and using information-gap activities, problem-solving tasks, and critical incidents (Wintergerst & McVeigh, 2011).

Critical incidents, in particular, consist of short stories or scenarios depicting cultural miscommunications that are vital for helping students to discover cultural dimensions. Students read and discuss these situations to identify the possible reasons for the miscommunication and ways to avoid it. These cross-cultural problematic situations can help students share fundamental elements of culture such as beliefs, values, norms, and opinions (Wintergerst & McVeigh, 2011). They may also enhance students' skills of discovery and interaction according to Byram's model.

In-class experiential learning activities, moreover, are recommended by Shin and Jeon (2018), who suggest a sample activity entitled *Nacirema* (the word "American" spelled backwards) that can be utilized with both pre- and in-service teachers. The teacher portrays the classroom as the lost island of Nacirema, which has been closed to outsiders for a long time. However, this island will now host some anthropologists. While 3–5 students take the role of these anthropologists, the others remain in the classroom and take on the role of island inhabitants. The "anthropologists" are told that they are being sent by the president of a university to explore this culture and then report to the president on a cultural topic such as greeting customs. They are asked to prepare questions and gather data in a creative way through 2-minute conversations. The teacher also informs the "inhabitants" about the cultural values and communication rules of Nacimerans, who then interact and answer the questions of the anthropologists. At the end of the process, in a whole-class discussion, both parties are asked critical and reflective questions about their experiences, feelings, and understandings (Shin & Jeon, 2018).

Drama is another in-class format for promoting intercultural awareness, allowing students to explore cultures or theatre traditions in other cultures and compare them with their own. For instance, an English play could be translated into another language to reflect the practices and perspectives of the new culture, while role-play exercises and improvisations help learners to explore aspects of both their own and other cultures. Drama allows students to assume a new identity, which may remove their inhibitions and allow them to act as both a participant and observer, bringing their real-life experiences to drama and creating new meanings from them (Fleming, 2003). Such activities have the potential to enhance the skills of interpreting, relating, discovery and interaction according to Byram's ICC model.

Multicultural literature provides yet another means to explore diverse cultures, encouraging learners to feel tolerance towards diversity and helping them to think critically, thereby enhancing their intercultural awareness and competence. Multicultural literature includes works on racial, ethnic, and social diversity and can be categorized as world literature, cross-cultural literature, and parallel culture literature. World literature, in this sense, refers to works produced by non-Western authors, whereas cross-cultural literature mainly focuses on cultural gaps and interrelationships. Parallel cultural literature, on the other hand, is produced by acculturated and socialized authors in a community representing cultural heritage (Chang, 2018).

The Out-of-Class Approach to Intercultural Awareness

As Cushner and Mahon (2009) note, intercultural competence cannot be developed via the cognitive approach alone. Rather, hands-on intercultural experience is a necessity for connecting the affective domain of students, whether they are school children or pre-service teachers, to their cognition. In other words:

> It is through impactful experiences, where people are challenged to make sense of their new environment and accommodate to the difference, where they ultimately gain more sophisticated knowledge about other people and a feeling of being at home in a new context. (Cushner & Mahon, 2009, p. 316)

International immersion experience is suggested as one of the most effective means for fostering critical intercultural competence outside the classroom. This involves a student teaching opportunity in which the intern provides instruction to classroom with students from diverse cultures, requiring them to learn to cope in an unfamiliar cultural context. One form of the immersion experience is community-based service learning, in which pre-service teachers practice teaching in a different community and then reflect on their experience. For example, in their small-scale case study in Toronto, ten pre-service Korean teachers taught Korean culture, as well as English, to Korean-Canadian students in a camp setting. This experience helped them improve their personal self-efficacy, sensitize them to both linguistic and cultural diversity, develop empathy for other people, and improve their teaching skills in general (Shin & Jeon, 2018).

To provide another example, in a mixed methods study with 8 pre-service teachers and alumni, Holland (2013) found that participants gained several benefits from an international experience. Their cultural adaptability improved in that they modified their way of thinking, enjoyed the process, behaved confidently, and empathized with their students. Self-presentation was a further benefit, in that they confidently presented their own identity in the classroom, thereby engaging their students and helping them learn different cultures. In addition, they developed tolerance for uncertainty in that they learned how to adjust and feel comfortable in an unfamiliar environment. Cultural engagement was found to be another benefit of the process, as the participants felt motivated to explore their new context, developed rapport with their students, and communicated with students from diverse linguistic and cultural backgrounds in a positive way. This attitude turned them into bridge builders between cultures. Still another benefit of this experience was determination, in that they were determined to achieve their teaching goals rather than give up on their attempt to connect with diverse students.

Similar positive outcomes have been reported in the Turkish context. Şahin (2008), for example, found that an international student teaching experience contributed to pre-service teachers' professional and personal development. In this case, they learned how to personalize their teaching, as well as to use technology effectively in their classrooms. In addition, this cross-cultural experience increased their self-confidence, developed their interpersonal skills, and increased their sense of responsibility. Their international experience also helped them to better understand not only American culture, but also Turkish culture, as well as improving their communication skills. Such international teaching projects for student teachers may enable them to design their own culture-oriented syllabi, as well as encouraging them to pursue academic degrees in culture-related fields, to become members of culture-related special interest groups, to attend related conferences, and to think and behave as an intercultural mediator despite institutional restrictions (Davcheva, 2003).

In addition to home-based intercultural encounters, overseas student teaching experiences are regarded as vital to raising culture-conscious language teachers. This may entail sending students to national schools in English-speaking countries or to international and bilingual schools in non-English countries, where they teach under the guidance of supervisors. They may be further exposed to the local culture by living with host families. This experience helps teachers grow as "globally minded" (Cushner & Chang, 2015, p. 2) agents, as they come to recognize the cultural diversity in their classrooms and in the community and to develop ideas about how to equip their own students with skills of collaborating with others and finding solutions for global problems.

Overseas teaching experiences have also been reported as contributing to speaking and communicative confidence, enhancing interpersonal skills, developing worldviews regarding culture, supporting appreciation for the worldviews of others, increasing global awareness, and aiding adaptation to a new working culture (Ateşkan, 2016). On the contrary, Cushner and Chang (2015) found in their study that it is not always realistic to expect significant changes by asking students live and teach on their own in other countries. Similarly, Salazar and Agüero (2016) found in their survey that a study-abroad experience had no significant effect on IC. In this regard, cognitive gains regarding interculturality are not seen as enough. Rather, attitudes and values need to change, and the new realization should be put into action; thus, although experience is a precondition, it does not ensure intercultural awareness. To achieve this, students need to be encouraged to reflect on and analyze their experience (Alred, Byram, & Fleming, 2003). Therefore, Cushner and Chang (2015) suggest that "teacher educators should apply what others in the field of study abroad have learned and be more strategic and mindful in how we both prepare overseas student teachers and work with them throughout the experience" (p. 11). Therefore, overseas student teaching experiences need to be standardized and formalized, and preservice teachers should be guided before, during, and after this experience with activities such as reflection and debriefing.

In addition to overseas teaching experiences, *short-term study visit programs* that offer cross-cultural experiences may also be useful in developing intercultural competence. To illustrate, Akpinar and Ünaldi (2014) compared the intercultural sensitivity levels of Turkish science and language teacher trainers after a mobility program. Although they found more significant changes in the science group, both parties' intercultural attitudes covering components such as knowledge, attitudes, skills, and awareness developed. Both groups learned to appreciate people from diverse cultures, to be open-minded, to analyze and recognize their own attitudes and knowledge about differences, to use language confidently and successfully in an international context, to observe people successfully, to eliminate their prejudices and biases, and to show tolerance and respect towards differences.

International student mobility programs such as Erasmus+ also have the potential to expose pre-service teachers to other cultures and increase their cultural awareness, as well as ensure professional development, particularly when teacher education programs do not offer culture-related courses. Such programs have led to major personal development outcomes. Ersoy and Günel (2011), for instance, have observed changes in world views; increased self-confidence regarding future teaching careers; greater attempts at interaction; broadened cultural knowledge and open-mindedness; enhanced curiosity about other cultures; and rejection of stereotypes about both local and world cultures. As students participate in mobility programs abroad, they also acquire strategic skills of learning how to live on their own and adapting their skills to a new culture. In addition, their self-confidence increases as they learn to cope with diversity-related issues and develop social competence and interpersonal skills through their encounters with others from diverse backgrounds. All these experiences turn them into more open-minded, tolerant, and flexible people with critical awareness of both themselves and others (Murphy-Lejeune, 2003), resulting in cognitive, linguistic and sociocultural growth.

An additional way to foster diversity is by carrying out *collaborative projects via technology*. Digital media, in particular, have great potential for enhancing intercultural awareness of both teachers and teacher candidates, as well as students, as they allow participants to engage in first-hand intercultural interactions in an online environment. For example, in Lázár's (2015) case study, four English teachers from Bulgaria, Hungary, Italy and Turkey conducted five-month-long international web collaboration projects with their 10th and 11th grade students. Although they initially had only superficial knowledge about both their own and the other cultures, at the end of the project, their intercultural awareness had improved significantly. They understood what was needed for successful intercultural communications, their observation and discovery skills were expanded, and their attitudes towards openness to and respect for others improved.

In Conclusion

Turkish society is diverse, not only due to its own rich multicultural heritage, but also as host to millions of refugees and foreign national residents. Hence, the field of English language education is expected to take proactive measures to address diversity, at least in terms of culture and intercultural awareness. This aim may be realized at universities, where teacher candidates are prepared personally and professionally for the teaching profession; and in schools, where practicing teachers are supported professionally. The recent initiatives of the CoHE, i.e., the curricular revisions to pre-service teacher education, are promising in that they aim to extend intercultural education to schools by training culturally sensitive language teachers.

Recently, as previously noted, the CoHE has begun to permit teacher education programs to include elective courses in addition to the prescribed course content, and some program coordinators have opted to include culture and diversity-related electives. However, without a unified approach, there is no means to ensure that such courses are actually equipping teacher candidates with the skills needed to manage diversity in the classroom. In order to respond to these concerns in the context of ITE, several recommendations can be made: (1) educational policy-makers should respond to ongoing calls to recognize the value and importance of cultural diversity and to include provisions for preparing teachers to cope with diversity; (2) standards for enrollment in teacher education programs should be raised, and the acceptance process should be more selective, in order to focus on training a smaller number of highly motivated and competent candidates; (3) case studies of existing diversity-related courses offered as electives in ITE programs should be carried out in order to determine whether they are successfully equipping pre-service teachers with the skills they need to cope with growing student diversity; recommendations for modifying and expanding these programs should be drawn from the results. Such studies may be seen as particularly important due to the rarity of these courses and the need to expand them to other programs; (4) teacher education curricula should be revised to include both coursework and fieldwork addressing learner diversity. Such courses should be required in all teacher training programs.

In closing, diversity via cultural intelligence must be fostered in teacher education in more ways than just learning facts about the traits that belong to diverse cultures. This involves awareness of self and others and attaining specific skills related to intercultural communicative competence. In this process, teacher educators should keep in mind that examining one's own culture is of utmost importance in fostering cultural awareness and intercultural competence. As Peterson (2004) advises, "use other cultures as a mirror to see your own" (p. 162).

References

Akpinar, K. D., & Ünaldi, I. (2014). Exploring intercultural competence in teacher education: A comparative study between science and foreign language teacher trainers. *Educational Research and Reviews, 9*(21), 1156–1164.

Alred, G., Byram, M., & Fleming, (2003). Introduction. In G. Alred, M. Byram, & M. Fleming (Eds.), *Intercultural experience and education* (pp. 1–13). Multilingual Matters.

Ateşkan, A. (2016). Pre-service teachers' cultural and teaching experiences abroad. *Journal of Education for Teaching, 42*(2), 135–148.

Aydın, S. (2016, May). Türkiye'de yabancı dil öğretmeni yetiştirme: Bir öneri [Foreign language teacher training in Turkey: A proposal]. Paper presented at the 4th National Conference on Foreign Language Education, Çanakkale Onsekiz Mart University, Çanakkale, Turkey.

Bektaş-Çetinkaya, Y., & Çelik, S. (2013). Perceptions of Turkish EFL teacher candidates on their level of intercultural competence. In H. Arslan & G. Raţă (Eds.), *Multicultural education: From theory to practice* (pp. 345–362). Cambridge Scholars Press.

Brislin, R. W. (2000). *Understanding culture's influence on behavior* (2nd ed.). Harcourt.

Byram, M. (1997). *Teaching and assessing intercultural communicative competence.* Multilingual Matters.

Chang, S.-C. (2018). *Assessing intercultural competence and exploring practices of multicultural literature among elementary language arts teachers* [Doctoral dissertation, Kent State University]. OhioLINK Educational ETD. http://rave.ohiolink.edu/etdc/view?acc_num=kent1517080175951363.

Cushner, K. (2007). The role of experience in the making of internationally-minded teachers. *Teacher Education Quarterly, 34*(1), 27–39.

Cushner, K. (2011). Intercultural research in teacher education: An essential intersection in the preparation of globally competent teachers. *Action in Teacher Education, 33*(5–6), 601–614.

Cushner, K., & Chang, S. C. (2015). Developing intercultural competence through overseas student teaching: Checking our assumptions. *Intercultural Education, 26*(3), 165–178.

Cushner, K., & Mahon, J. (2009). Intercultural competence in teacher education: Developing the intercultural competence of educators and their students. In D. K. Deardorff (Ed.), *The SAGE handbook of intercultural competence* (pp. 304–320). SAGE.

Çelik, S. (2013). Plurilingualism, pluriculturalism, and the CEFR: Are Turkey's foreign language objectives reflected in classroom instruction? *Procedia Social and Behavioral Sciences, 70,* 1872–1879.

Çelik, S. (2014a). Classroom strategies of Turkish EFL teachers in managing cultural diversity. In P. Romanowski (Ed.), *Intercultural issues in the era of globalization* (pp. 32–46). Wydawnictwo Naukowe.

Çelik, S. (2014b, May). Towards the need for a hands-on approach to teaching foreign cultures in the EFL classroom. In *Proceedings of the International Conference on Language, Literature and Culture in Education (LLCE2014), Nitra, Slovakia* (pp. 188–193).

Çelik, S. (2016). Setting new standards for in-service teacher training: A model for responsive professional development in the context of English language teaching. In K. Dikilitaş & İ. H. Erten (Eds.), *Facilitating in-service teacher training for professional development* (pp. 300–310). IGI Global.

Çelik, S. (2017, May). In the discussion on "doing diversity" in education, how do English language teaching programs measure up? Paper presented at the 4th annual Conference on Sustainable Multilingualism: Language, Culture and Society, Kaunas, Lithuania.

Çelik, S., & Erbay, Ş. (2013). Cultural perspectives of Turkish ELT coursebooks: Do standardized teaching texts incorporate intercultural features? *Education and Science, 38*(167), 336–351.

Çelik, S., & Gül Peker, B. (2019). The CEFR and English language teaching: A framework for communicative competence. In İ. Yaman, E. Ekmekçi, & M. Şenel (Eds.), *Basics of ELT* (pp. 480–509). Blackswan Publishing House.

Çelik, S., & Karaca, B. (2014, May). Considering culture in developing an EFL curriculum for K-8 learners in Turkey. In *Proceedings of the International Conference on Language, Literature and Culture in Education (LLCE2014), Nitra, Slovakia* (pp. 168–175).

Çelik, Ş. N., & Kasap, S. (2019). Türkiye'de uygulanan İngilizce öğretmen yetiştirme programları üzerine karşılaştırmalı bir değerlendirme [A comparative evaluation of English teacher training programs implemented in Turkey]. Van Yuzuncu Yıl University *Journal of Education, 16*(1), 1010–1031.

Davcheva, L. (2003). Learning to be intercultural. In G. Alred, M. Byram, & M. Fleming (Eds.), *Intercultural experience and education* (pp. 67–86). Multilingual Matters.

Deardorff, D. K. (2011). Assessing intercultural competence. *New Directions for Institutional Research, 149,* 65–79.

Ersoy, A., & Günel, E. (2011). Cross-cultural experiences through Erasmus: Pre-service teachers' individual and professional development. *Eurasian Journal of Educational Research, 42,* 63–78.

Fleming, M. (2003). Intercultural experience and drama. In G. Alred, M. Byram, & M. Fleming (Eds.), *Intercultural experience and education* (pp. 87–100). Multilingual Matters.

Hofstede, G. (1991). *Cultures and organizations: Software of the mind.* McGraw-Hill.

Holland, C. K. (2013). *Classroom intercultural competence in teacher education students, interns, and alumni* [Doctoral dissertation, University of North Florida]. UNF Digital Commons. https://digitalcommons.unf.edu/cgi/viewcontent.cgi?article=1495&context=etd.

Kahraman, A. (2016). Teachers' and learners' attitudes towards culture and culture learning in a Turkish context. *Journal of Language and Linguistic Studies, 12*(2), 1–12.

Karakaş, A. (2012). Evaluation of the English language teacher education program in Turkey. *ELT Weekly, 4*(15), 1–16.

Lázár, I. (2015). EFL learners' intercultural competence development in an international web collaboration project. *The Language Learning Journal, 43*(2), 208–221.

Ministry of National Education (MoNE). (2017). Teacher strategy paper 2017–2023. https://oygm.meb.gov.tr/meb_iys_dosyalar/2018_05/25170118_Teacher_Strategy_Paper_2017-2023.pdf.

Murphy-Lejeune, E. (2003). An experience of interculturality: Student travelers abroad. In G. Alred, M. Byram, & M. Fleming (Eds.), *Intercultural experience and education* (pp. 101–113). Multilingual Matters.

Önalan, O. (2005). EFL teachers' perceptions of the place of culture in ELT: A survey study at four universities in Ankara/Turkey. *Journal of Language and Linguistic Studies, 1*(2), 215–235.

Öztürk, G., & Aydın, B. (2019). English language teacher education in Turkey: Why do we fail and what policy reforms are needed? *Anadolu Journal of Educational Sciences, 9*(1), 181–213.

Pena-Dix, B. M. (2018). *Developing intercultural competence in English language teachers: Towards building intercultural language education in Colombia.* [Doctoral dissertation, Durham University]. Durham e-Theses. http://etheses.dur.ac.uk/12619/1/21-05-2018-Beatriz_Pe%C3%B1a_Dix_THESIS.pdf?DDD29+.

Peterson, B. (2004). *Cultural intelligence: A guide to working with people from other cultures.* Intercultural Press.

Salazar, M. G., & Agüero, M. F. (2016). Intercultural competence in teaching: Defining the intercultural profile of student teachers. *Bellaterra Journal of Teaching & Learning Language & Literature, 9*(4), 41–58.

Shin, H., & Jeon, M. (2018). Intercultural competence and critical English language teacher education. *English Teaching, 73*(4), 125–147.

Spitzberg, B. H., & Changnon, G. (2009). Conceptualizing intercultural competence. In D. K. Deardorff (Ed.), *The SAGE handbook of intercultural competence (pp.* 2–52). SAGE.

Şahin, M. (2008). Cross-cultural experience in preservice teacher education. *Teaching and Teacher Education, 24*(7), 1777–1790.

Tarman, B. (2010). Global perspectives and challenges in teacher education in Turkey. *International Journal of Arts and Sciences, 3*(17), 78–96.

T.C. Yükseköğretim Kurulu (YÖK) [Higher Education Council (CoHE)]. (2018). *İngilizce öğretmenliği lisans programı.* https://www.yok.gov. tr/Documents/Kurumsal/egitim_ogretim_dairesi/Yeni-Ogretmen-Yetistirme-Lisans-Programlari/Ingilizce_Ogretmenligi_Lisans_Programi. pdf.

Thapa, S. (2020). Assessing intercultural competence in teacher education: A missing link. In H. M. Westerlund, S. Karlsen, & H. Partti (Eds.), *Visions for intercultural music teacher education* (pp. 163–176). Springer.

The Council of Higher Education (CoHE). (2014). *Higher education system in Turkey.* CoHE.

Tongal, Ç. (2015). Intercultural education in Turkey: From the rhetoric of "cultural mosaic" to the acknowledgement of diversity in classrooms. In A. Küppers & Ç. Bozdağ (Eds.), *Doing diversity in education through multilingualism, media and mobility* (pp. 15–17). Istanbul Policy Centre.

Uysal, H. H. (2012). Evaluation of an in-service training program for primary-school language teachers in Turkey. *Australian Journal of Teacher Education, 37*(7), 14–29.

Uztosun, M. S. (2018). In-service teacher education in Turkey: English language teachers' perspectives. *Professional Development in Education, 44*(4), 557–569.

Weaver, G. R. (1986). Understanding and coping with cross-cultural adjustment stress. In R. M. Paige (Ed.), *Cross-cultural orientation. New conceptualizations and applications* (pp. 111–145). University Press of America.

Wintergerst, A. C., & McVeigh, J. (2011). *Tips for teaching culture: Practical approaches to intercultural communication.* Pearson Education.

Yazıcı, S., Başol, G., & Toprak, G. (2009). Teachers' attitudes toward multicultural education: A Study of reliability and validity. *Hacettepe University Journal of Education, 37*, 229–242.

Yüksel, İ. (2012). The current developments in teacher education in Turkey on the threshold of [the] European Union. *International Journal of Humanities and Social Science, 2*(8), 49–56.

Eda Nur Özcan and Esim Gürsoy

3   The Representation of Culture into ELT Materials

Introduction

"A language is a part of a culture and a culture is a part of a language; the two are intricately interwoven so that one cannot separate the two without losing the significance of either language or culture"

(Brown, 1994, p. 165)

"A study of language solely as an abstract system would not equip learners to use it in the real world"

(Cunningsworth, 1995, p. 86)

"Outdoor gardens with no meaning in themselves unless they are related to and contrasted with indoor apartments and dwellings"

(Kramsch, 2013, p. 71)

It is a known fact that language cannot be taught without culture. Thus, one of the main goals of language pedagogy has recently become the integration of culture into English Language Teaching (ELT) materials and the integration has become increasingly more essential for the spreading role of English language in the world. Seeing that teaching English and teaching culture is inseparable, adopting the materials accordingly seems to have considerable importance. However, there is a misconception that foreign language materials should heavily reflect the culture of target language. Today this misbelief is about to vanish because for several decades the English language seems to have belonged to whomever speaks it.

The emergence of Kachruvian Model, which will be discussed in this chapter, led a paradigm shift in the ELT world. Therefore, the ownership of English is shared by many nations. Many language learners are coming from diverse backgrounds and the numbers show that there are more non-native speakers of English than native speakers of English. The recognition of diversity has brought out novelty, such as; the need to know about other cultures because people from different backgrounds interact and they have one thing in common, that is English, by using this common language, people are expected to communicate with each other and the interaction requires knowledge and awareness on intercultural basis. Simply put, teaching culture has become a must in English language classrooms and thus, it must be reflected in ELT materials according to the new status of English as a lingua franca. Within the scope of this chapter, ELT coursebooks will be the focal point as it is the most common material used in ELT classrooms today and coursebooks, as they offer various contents and illustrations, have potential to shape learners' way of thinking. Before we go deeper in discussing the integration of culture into ELT materials, it is important to define what culture means and how it is defined in the relevant literature.

What Is Culture?

Culture as a concept might be highly complex to define. According to Kramsch & Widdowson (1998), culture means being a member in a community which holds the same historical background, physical space and common mental images. Hinkel (1999) puts forward more critical definition of culture as searching for knowledge about a society, the groups in a society, the systems emerged by a society and people's behaviors within the systems. However, these definitions seem to evaluate culture in a general sense. To offer more detailed definition of the concept, referring to Liddicoat, Papademetre, Scarino and Kohler (2003) might be more helpful in order to deepen in the definition of culture. Liddicoat et al. (2003) discuss culture as a sophisticated area in which the cognitive and behavioral presence of human is included as well as the institutions that are created and the products that are produced by them. Behavioral presence implies practices, lifestyles and rituals of the culture group whereas cognitive presence implies values, attitudes and interests of the specific group. So as to elaborate on such a complex concept, the need to narrow down the definition of culture has emerged in the relevant literature.

Lee (2009) posits that culture reflecting the facts regarding history, geography, education, customs and arts, which belongs to a certain society, can be named as Big Culture (Big C). Peterson (2004) adds that Big C covers big themes such as classic products of the society like music, literature and architecture. Shortly, core values, regardless of being abstract or concrete, concerns Big C. On the other hand, Little Culture (Little C) focuses on daily aspects of life in a certain speech community. Unlike big themes in Big C, Little C targets minor themes such as perspectives of people in the society, cuisine, the way of dressing, body language, hobbies etc. (Peterson, 2004). See the table below for examples of Big C and Little C in U.S. culture (Center for Open Educational Resources & Language Learning, 2020).

Examples of Big C	Examples of Little C
The Great Depression	a MacDonald's menu
Independence Day (July 4th)	a bus ticket
The Great Gatsby	iPods
The White House	Baseball

Taking Cortazzi and Jin's (1999) claims about culture into consideration, culture can be examined in three different dimensions as target culture, international culture and home culture. The concept of target culture includes the cultures in which English is the mother tongue such as UK, The USA, Canada, Ireland, New Zealand and Australia. As Jahan and Roger (2006) stated, they reflect the culture both traditionally and linguistically. The countries where English language is seen as ESL/EFL or, in other words, the countries that are defined as being in the outer Circle and the expanding Circle by Kachru (1985) are categorized as international culture and in a Turkish context; Turkish culture is categorized or defined as home culture. These categories are essential for material evaluation since they provide a concrete conceptual framework for investigation. However, such a distinction might be wrong today because globalization of the world is becoming faster than ever and a common world culture is about to occur as a result of it. See the table below for examples of Target Culture, International Culture and Home Culture.

Target Culture	International Culture	Home Culture
Fish & Chips in England	Bullfighting in Spain	Turkish Coffee
The Statue of Liberty in U. S	Chinese New Year	Turkish Bath

Teaching Culture and Implications for ELT Materials

Paradigm Shift in Teaching Culture

There has been a common belief for many years in the field of Applied Linguistics and that is the role of English in the world. In late 1970s, the concept of World Englishes took its place thanks to contributions of Kachru (1976). He argued that there are many varieties of English as well as British varieties and American varieties so we need to appreciate other varieties as they contribute to the English language in the globalized English-speaking world. Ten years after his

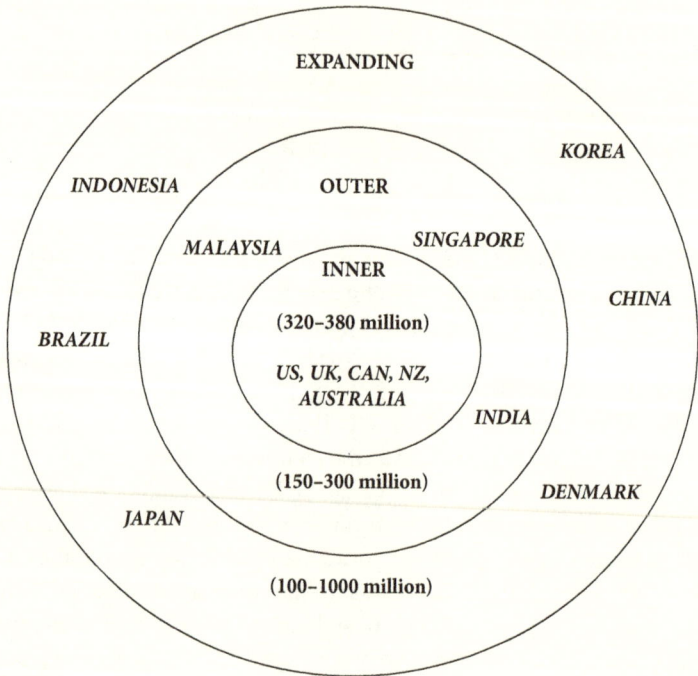

Fig. 1: Kachru's Three Circles Model (1985)

claim, Kachru (1985) proposed a model (see Fig. 1) in which he describes the status of English in the world. In his three circles model, he named the circles from inner to outer as norm providing, norm developing and norm dependent. However, Jenkins (2006) posits that the outer circle is not norm dependent; on the contrary, the outer circle constructs specific varieties. This view has been named as plurilingualism and has become a popular research subject in the field. Plurilingualism as a popular research area has proved that target varieties and cultures cannot be the focus of English language teaching alone; therefore, the co-occurrence of other languages in English language teaching has started to be appreciated. This view led a paradigm shift in language education since plurilingualism paves the way for multiculturalism. Therefore, ELT materials are expected to reflect multicultural elements in their contents.

The fact that English is an international language should be reflected in materials. When Kachru's circles are taken into consideration, one of the ways to do so is not to limit the contents of the materials to the target language. Alptekin

(2002) claims that culture that is taught should be the culture of the world and it should not be restricted with one or two. In Turkey, many things have changed about English language teaching since Turkey's membership to the Council of Europe (CoE) in 1949 and with the adoption of the Common European Framework of Reference (CEFR) and European Language Portfolio (ELP). Now that CEFR determines the path to follow in ELT Turkey has been trying to keep up with CEFR since 2006 (Çelik & Erbay, 2013). As a result of these efforts, multi-culturalism is expected to take much attention in instructional design. However, some studies have shown that Turkey has failed to follow the standards of CEFR in instructional design (Büyükkantarcıoğlu, 2004; Kırkgöz, 2009). Elements presented in the government-issued ELT coursebooks have been found to be narrow in terms of representing intercultural diversity (Özcan, 2020). Research has revealed that local culture is the focus in Turkey's ELT coursebooks and the representations of common cultural practices are very frequent in the books (Çakır, 2010; Cortazzi & Jin, 1999). As a similar research, Çelik and Erbay (2013) conducted an investigation on a government-issued series of three books to see if the cultural content is limited or not by focusing on the cultural elements from four different aspects as products, people, perspectives and practices. They concluded that the coursebooks take multicultural diversity into consideration while representing the language; however, they discovered a tendency about the European culture. Yet still, the findings are significant when the findings of other related studies are taken into account as they stated vice versa.

Importance of Teaching Culture in ELT classrooms

Teachers of English are traditionally prone to ignore the importance of cultural knowledge in their classrooms. There is a tendency to believe that foreign language communication is mainly made up of the application of grammatical rules to spoken and written production.

> The orthodox views of language teaching that sees language as a linguistic code are no longer the sole perception of language educators due to the shift in education theory toward intercultural understanding, the responsibility of the language educator has also expanded. (Gürsoy, 2014, p. 66)

Despite the expanded responsibility of language educators, teaching culture is often neglected in language classrooms. A close interaction with people from a different culture does not happen so often and thus, learners cannot understand the importance of learning culture unless they have experience about it. For learners, the most common way of exposure to culture is TV series or movies. However, these contents may invoke misunderstandings about certain cultures from time to time; therefore, unbiased teaching and representation of culture in ELT materials are necessary. McKay (2004) explains the influence of culture into ELT contexts in two different dimensions. The linguistic dimension covers semantics, pragmatics and discourses of language while the pedagogical dimension covers the choice of language and materials including cultural content. In this particular chapter, the focus is on the pedagogical dimension. As to CEFR, the promotion of the world peace and the understanding at an international level can be provided through teaching intercultural awareness. It is the main reason why language curricula should contain intercultural elements (Kitao, 1991). In addition, international understanding, learning and teaching cultures make language learning more meaningful, provide authentic materials, help learners not to hold bias and diminish ambiguity.

Various advantages that come with culture teaching and learning have helped it to be called as "the fifth skill". Yet still, it is apparent that teachers of English mostly depend on teaching Big Culture when it is time to teach culture as the fifth skill. It is not only because teachers are not equipped with enough knowledge about Big or Little Culture, but also marketing concerns of ELT materials push teachers to do so. Finding cultural examples aiming to Big Culture is easier from the point of coursebook producers and seeing that these cultural examples are well-known, it can be guaranteed that students are able to comprehend them faster. However, the discussion starts at this point. Should culture be used as being only a subject matter (a reading passage, a listening audio including a traveller's experience abroad) in ELT materials? Or should it contribute to learners' acquisition of language linguistically and the integration of learners with the rest of the world for making them internalize the main objective of language learning (communication) and to reflect on their own culture for establishing a "sphere of inter-culturality" (Kramsch, 1993). If you prefer the latter one as a cultural objective in your classroom, then you probably need to provide the development of the following skills that are helpful for enhancing intercultural competence (Choudhury, 2013, p. 23) in your classroom.

- Asking questions about cultures.
- Listening and seeking clarifications.
- Negotiating and identifying common grounds.
- Avoiding prejudging or stereotyping.

As a teacher, you can also integrate Cultural Facts Approach proposed by Sowa's (2014) into your language classrooms. This approach can lead your students to look from a wider perspective into different cultures while internalizing not only big cultural products, but also little cultural products. It is important to note, while following any cultural approaches, the flow of the lesson should include discussion (Chlopek, 2008).

Sowa's (2014) Cultural Facts Approach

- When it is time to teach culture, try to focus on little culture products more.
- Help your students see similarities and differences amongst cultures.
- Cultural knowledge and showing positive attitudes matter.
- Talk about facts not about stereotypes.

Representation of Culture in ELT Materials

The most common material used for English language teaching is coursebooks; many language teachers plan their lessons depending on them. Masuhara and Tomlinson (2008) highlights the dependence on coursebooks might lead failure of students since many coursebooks lack contents which have potential to initiate meaningful communication requiring intercultural competence. Inadequate contents of coursebooks result from the approach named "teaching to the test" and thus, coursebooks have a tendency to neglect intercultural elements within their body (Byram & Feng, 2004). However, intercultural elements have been indispensable parts of language teaching since 1970s when English was started to be taught for communicative purposes. The fact that English is the global language requires us to make the culture teaching process neutral. In this case, teaching English-speaking cultures will not be appropriate as the learners will use English to communicate in cross cultural environments (Alptekin, 2002).

The Representation of Culture in International Coursebooks

As well as the diverse representation of culture in the coursebooks, the manner of representation bears importance. Yuen (2011) argues the cultural contents in coursebooks are often normalized and generalized. They, in fact, lack real and rich examples, thereby causing bias in target audience. As mentioned earlier, this is also one of the results of marketability of ELT products. Commercial purposes lead coursebooks to follow a "one size fits all" approach (Gray, 2002). Therefore, general facts about certain cultures draw interest in many coursebooks in the world, which prevents diversity and culture teaching in general. It often means that coursebooks hardly include little culture elements. Rodríguez (2015) defines Big C and Little C with different terms as surface culture and deep culture. His investigation on coursebooks shows that materials are prone to present surface culture elements such as the achievement of celebrities, food, tourist attractions etc., however these are too general facts and they cannot equip learners with necessary cultural information that they need for acculturated language learning process. From this point of view, cultural content in coursebooks seem to have tourist-friendly approach. Therefore, language learners are treated as if they were "superficial tourists who travel from one country to another without any serious engagement with those cultures" (Liddicoat & Scarino, 2013). Relating the Spanish with bullfighting, the English with fish and chips and the Italians with pizza in coursebooks are extremely common and resembles to a tourist guide book. Integration of language and culture should go further than representing iconic elements (Troncoso, 2010).

Global coursebooks are mostly produced by the western societies and it is seen that values and beliefs represented in these coursebooks belong to the western societies again (Kumaravadivelu, 2008). From another standpoint, commercial purposes forces publishers to produce Anglo-centric coursebooks for the market, which means English-speaking culture is dominant within the coursebooks (Nomnian, 2013). Publishers succumb to misconception that target culture is of primary importance. For example, in one study examining two English coursebooks used by Hong Kong secondary schools, Yuen (2011) found that the coursebooks preferred to present English-speaking cultures while African culture is underrepresented. Ke (2012) published a comprehensive study on English coursebooks used in Taiwan and stated that Anglo-American were dominant from 1925 to 2009 but it seems that this dominance started to decline since 2009 and now the coursebooks shift their attention to the world culture. Silvia (2015) examined two English coursebooks used in high schools of Indonesia and found: Even though target culture, home culture and international culture were even in terms of the quantity of representation, the findings are not balanced qualitatively. Shin, Eslami and Chen (2011) similarly reported that the inner circle of Kachruvian model dominates in the coursebooks. Another study conducted by Kim and Paek (2015) from Korea stated that there was an imbalance in the representation of cultures in five different ELT coursebooks and the coursebooks favor Little C when the focus is on home culture.

In a nutshell, the studies conducted on ELT coursebooks in the world conclude that imbalance is very frequent both in terms of the source of culture (home, target, international) and the breath of culture (Big C, Small C). To be able to contribute to adequate culture teaching and language learning, imbalances in cultural contents of ELT coursebooks should be revisited and teachers are suggested to be selective in deciding on coursebooks. Details about selecting coursebooks will be discussed in the following parts of the chapter.

The Representation of Culture in National Coursebooks

The content analysis conducted on many coursebooks used worldwide shows that English coursebooks do not efficiently support culture teaching as they inevitably represent some bias or they lack certain features in providing necessary knowledge to learners in culture teaching process. All in all, many coursebooks that have been examined so far seem to be one-sided in that they give more room to only one aspect in terms of the breath of culture and the source of culture. To simply put, coursebooks mostly include Big Culture elements and by doing so, they primarily aim to teach target culture, which is a highly traditional approach to culture teaching. In Turkey, English lessons at private or state schools are generally followed by a syllabus included in a coursebook. The marked tendency for the use of coursebooks in Turkey is that private schools use mainstream ELT coursebooks, namely those published by Oxford, Cambridge, Macmillan etc. while public schools utilize the national coursebooks published and distributed by the Ministry of National Education. We believe that sharing results regarding the analysis of cultural findings in national coursebooks can portray the real situation of culture teaching in Turkey and can enlighten the way to revise our lessons according to the cultural needs of our students. The reason why this section is allocated to the analysis of national coursebooks is that these coursebooks address a great number of audiences.

The ministry of National Education has been giving lots of efforts to integrate CEFR features to its body for more than a decade. In 2013, curricula of English lessons were revisited and integrations based on the principles of CEFR were added. Accordingly, revisiting coursebooks was a part of this process (Cephe & Aşık, 2016). Yet still, the objectives that the ministry has held in this respect seem not to be fully attained as many studies, so far, have concluded that inadequacies are overtly seen in the representation of home, target and international culture and culture-neutral elements dominate the national coursebooks written by Turkish authors (Arslan, 2016; Başal, 2012; Çelik & Erbay, 2013; Demirbaş, 2013; Işık, 2011). However, we, either as practitioners or researchers, should always bear in mind that developing a multicultural approach to teach culture is essential (Cortezzi, 2000).

Previous studies showed that monocultural approach was more common. Siddique (2011) stated that *Spot Light on English*, a national ELT coursebook, heavily represents local culture while Çalman (2017) stated that *Yes You Can A1.2* represents international culture more, yet still he maintains that there is a balanced distribution in terms of the sources of culture. Yaman (2017) analyzed the same coursebook and he yielded the same findings as Çalman (2017).

Additionally, Çalman (2017) argues that 9th grade English Coursebook has a home-culture-based orientation. Such findings prove that there is no consensus in planning process of material development. Besides, Çalman (2017) exemplifies the cultural elements shown in both of the coursebooks and it is seen that Big Culture elements were used predominantly but such a discussion is beyond the scope of his research paper. Ulum and Bada (2016) made more detailed content analysis on the same book series *Yes You Can*, they examined 9 coursebooks by dividing cultural elements into two concrete categories as inner cultural elements and outer cultural elements. Their findings suggested that outer cultural elements were employed in the national coursebooks up to 68 percent. As seen above, Turkish literature on government-issued coursebooks are still premature.

Existing literature generally evaluate coursebooks depending the source of the culture, which states that the quantity of the elements has been being discussed for a while whereas the quality of the elements seems to be neglected. However, few studies suggested that coursebooks do not represent enough cultural elements, for example, idioms and superstitions, thus it can be concluded that these contents cannot lead students to acquire fully developed language competence (Çakır, 2010). Çelik and Erbay (2013) analyzed *Spot on 6, 7, 8 series* and argued that cultural products and persons are represented more but there is little place allocated to cultural practices and perspectives. In terms of the source of culture, Çelik and Erbay (2013) stated that there is no remarkable quantitative difference in the representation of culture even though the findings suggest that home culture elements outnumber other types from time to time.

In general, coursebook series, especially after 2012 with the new alignments to the national curriculum, try to adopt a balanced fashion in integrating culture into their contents and lead teachers to use cultural information (Gürsoy, 2014). This might result from Turkey's efforts to keep up with CEFR objectives. Özcan (2020) has recently investigated eight government-issued coursebooks distributed for 2018–2019 academic year. In her analysis, both the sources of culture and the breadth of culture were taken into account. She argues that each coursebook has a different approach while representing the source of culture as no common and generalizable finding has been attained. Home, target and international cultural elements are included in the coursebooks; however, the number of elements vary from one coursebook to another coursebook. However, it might have resulted from the fact that these coursebooks do not belong to any series like the other coursebook analysis mentioned above. To be able to get more information about the quality of cultural elements, the analysis of Big C and Little C has been incorporated into the investigation and it was found that the coursebooks are inclined to expose students to Big Culture elements more.

Tick (✔) the quotation/proverb below that best describes friendship in your opinion. Then share the quotations/proverbs about friendship in Turkish.

☐ Friends show their love in times of trouble, not in happiness. *(Euripides)*

☐ Don't walk behind me; I may not lead. Don't walk in front of me; I may not follow. Just walk beside me and be my friend. *(Albert Camus)*

☐ Walking with a friend in the dark is better than walking alone in the light. *(Helen Keller)*

☐ You never really know your friends from your enemies until the ice breaks. *(Eskimo Proverb)*

☐ The road to a friend's house is never long. *(Danish Proverb)*

Fig. 2: (taken from Upswing English) (Tıraş, 2018)

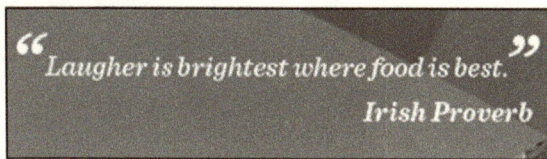

" *Laugher is brightest where food is best.* "
Irish Proverb

Fig. 3: (taken from Mastermind) (Çavuşer-Özdemir, Çavuşer-Yünlü, İlter, İzgi, & Yeter-Türkeri, 2018).

This finding suggests that integration of culture into ELT materials still need further research in Turkey. By looking back to the findings suggested in the past; coursebooks once densely employed the home culture elements and familiar cultural practices (Cortazzi & Jin, 1999), it can be concluded that the multicultural perspectives in developing coursebooks might have been recently adopted; however representing only familiar cultural issues is still an on-going problem.

Examples of Cultural Representations from National Coursebooks

In the extracts given below, you can find the examples of cultural representations from the coursebooks used in Turkish state schools.

Fig. 2 represents examples from the target and international cultures and all of them are examples of small culture.

Fig. 3 represents an example from the target culture and small culture.

WORLD EDUCATION NEWS

Turkey, Tuesday, March, 12, 2019   Special Edition   Issue 8900230(

Japanese Small Hands at Cleaning

There is an old school tradition in Japan. Japanese students clean their own classrooms by themselves instead of a janitor. The Japanese think it is very important for moral responsibility. Students take off their shoes when they enter their schools and wear slippers to keep their classrooms clean. They sweep the leaves in the garden, dust the shelves and take out the trash. All students share duties and do it periodically. They learn to respect themselves and the others. They keep their schools clean as their houses. If a student leaves his/ her desk dirty, the student on duty warns him/ her to clean the desk. In time, these responsibilities become a habit. This affects students' characteristic features and get them ready for the real world.

Fig. 4: (taken from Mastermind) (Çavuşer-Özdemir, et al. 2018).

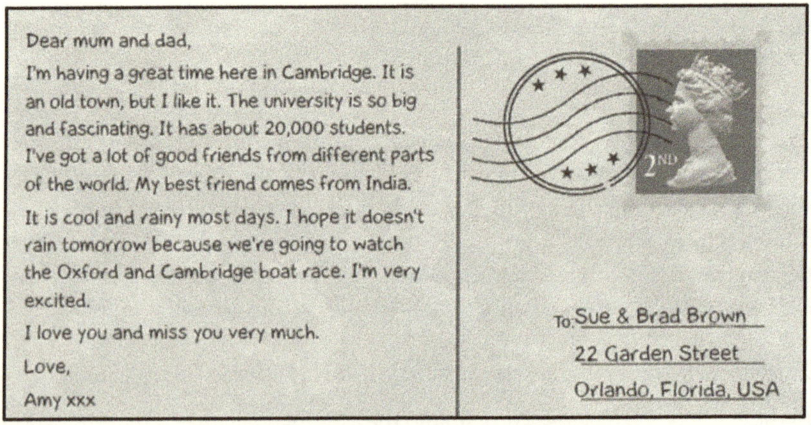

Dear mum and dad,

I'm having a great time here in Cambridge. It is an old town, but I like it. The university is so big and fascinating. It has about 20,000 students. I've got a lot of good friends from different parts of the world. My best friend comes from India.

It is cool and rainy most days. I hope it doesn't rain tomorrow because we're going to watch the Oxford and Cambridge boat race. I'm very excited.

I love you and miss you very much.

Love,

Amy xxx

To Sue & Brad Brown
22 Garden Street
Orlando, Florida, USA

Fig. 5: (taken from Relearn!) (Kaldar-Birincioğlu & Karamil (2019)

Fig. 6: (taken from Mastermind) (Çavuşer-Özdemir, et al. 2018).

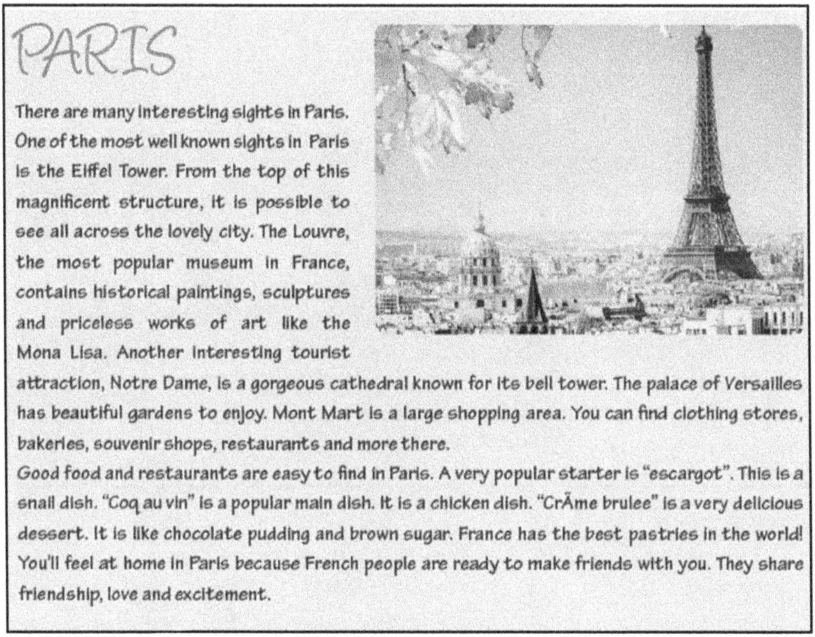

PARIS

There are many interesting sights in Paris. One of the most well known sights in Paris is the Eiffel Tower. From the top of this magnificent structure, it is possible to see all across the lovely city. The Louvre, the most popular museum in France, contains historical paintings, sculptures and priceless works of art like the Mona Lisa. Another interesting tourist attraction, Notre Dame, is a gorgeous cathedral known for its bell tower. The palace of Versailles has beautiful gardens to enjoy. Mont Mart is a large shopping area. You can find clothing stores, bakeries, souvenir shops, restaurants and more there.

Good food and restaurants are easy to find in Paris. A very popular starter is "escargot". This is a snail dish. "Coq au vin" is a popular main dish. It is a chicken dish. "Crême brulee" is a very delicious dessert. It is like chocolate pudding and brown sugar. France has the best pastries in the world! You'll feel at home in Paris because French people are ready to make friends with you. They share friendship, love and excitement.

Fig. 7: (taken from Relearn!) (Kaldar-Birincioğlu & Karamil (2019)

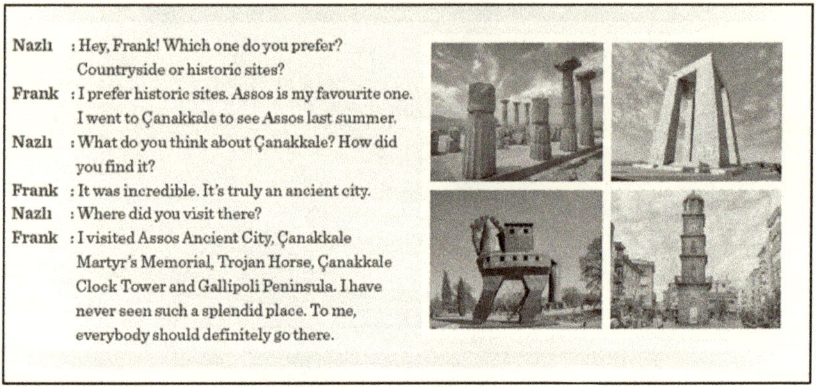

Nazlı : Hey, Frank! Which one do you prefer?
         Countryside or historic sites?
Frank : I prefer historic sites. Assos is my favourite one.
         I went to Çanakkale to see Assos last summer.
Nazlı : What do you think about Çanakkale? How did
         you find it?
Frank : It was incredible. It's truly an ancient city.
Nazlı : Where did you visit there?
Frank : I visited Assos Ancient City, Çanakkale
         Martyr's Memorial, Trojan Horse, Çanakkale
         Clock Tower and Gallipoli Peninsula. I have
         never seen such a splendid place. To me,
         everybody should definitely go there.

Fig. 8: (taken from Mastermind) (Çavuşer-Özdemir, et al. 2018).

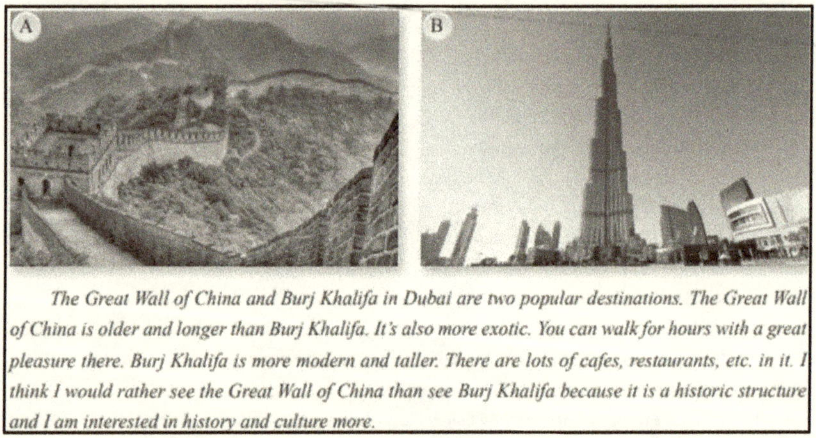

The Great Wall of China and Burj Khalifa in Dubai are two popular destinations. The Great Wall of China is older and longer than Burj Khalifa. It's also more exotic. You can walk for hours with a great pleasure there. Burj Khalifa is more modern and taller. There are lots of cafes, restaurants, etc. in it. I think I would rather see the Great Wall of China than see Burj Khalifa because it is a historic structure and I am interested in history and culture more.

Fig. 9: (taken from Upswing English) (Tiraş, 2018)

Fig. 4 represents an example from the international culture and small culture.
Fig. 5 represents an example from the target culture and small culture.
Fig. 6 represents an example from the home culture and small culture.
Fig. 7 represents the international culture and both small and big culture.
Fig. 8 represents an example from the home culture and big culture.
Fig. 9 represents an example from the international culture and big culture.

Culture in Coursebook Evaluation Checklist

When coursebooks are mentioned, there is one more thing that we certainly mention. To be able to evaluate coursebooks from various perspectives, checklists are great evaluation tools both for practitioners and researchers. They enable us to evaluate coursebooks effectively and practically. Cunningsworth (1995) claims, the most important aspect of a checklist is its being economic and systematic in that one can find many features in one list that matter for our language course. However, it is seen that many teachers do not refer to any checklists when it comes to the selection of the coursebooks; rather coursebooks seem to be chosen randomly (Ghorbani, 2011). It is essential to note that evaluation checklists are great helpers.

Evaluation checklists depend on the result of various studies in the field of applied linguistics and many checklists can be found in the relevant literature (Abdelwahab, 2013; Byrd, 2001; Cunningsworth, 1995; Daoud & Celce-Murcia, 1979; Garinger, 2002; Ghorbani, 2011; Halliwell, 1992; Litz, 2005; Ramzjoo, 2010; Skierso, 1991; Tekir & Arıkan, 2007; Williams, 1983). Demir and Ertaş (2014) evaluated 23 different coursebook evaluation checklists published between 1983 and 2014 and suggested an eclectic coursebook evaluation checklist (see appendix). Depending on their analysis, only two statements about culture emerged in these checklists; one of the statements is whether the content in the coursebook involve the target language culture and the other is whether the topics involve elements from home culture and target culture. The first statement takes its place in all of the checklists under the investigation but the latter one is found only in five of them. Based on the findings of this study, we can suggest that checklists need revising as more statements regarding the integration of culture into ELT materials can be added. No statement is seen about international culture elements, which is a desperate need as we are teaching our students to communicate in a globalized world.

Beside the source of the culture, what kind of culture (Small Culture or Big Culture) is integrated into coursebooks is a serious issue as not every culture element is adequate enough to support language acquisition linguistically and pedagogically. Finally, whether cultural elements can cause bias or not can be another statement to discuss in the selection of coursebooks. The statements regarding discriminations or prejudices exist, however these statements are not specified with cultural elements. Following statements for coursebook evaluation checklists can be suggestions for teachers while selecting a coursebook or they can be implications for further research.

- Does the content serve as a window into learning about the target culture?
- Does the content serve as a window into learning about the home culture?

- Does the content serve as a window into learning about the international culture?
- Is the distribution of cultural elements amongst the target, the home and the international culture equal?
- Does the cultural content represent both well-known products of society (art, music, literature etc.) and daily aspects of life in the society (dressing, habits, values etc.)?
- Is the cultural content free from cultural stereotypes (e.g., the British are cold, the French never speak English with tourists etc.)?

Conclusions

Teaching a language does not only mean teaching the ability of speaking, it also means teaching how to speak in a specific content. Culture involves primary contextual clues in all conversations as language is shaped by culture and culture is shaped by language. This circle is highly dynamic seeing that language is a living organism that constantly renews itself. This position of language indicates the significance of "*understanding of culture*". The globalization of the world requires the skills for intercultural awareness and intercultural awareness gives birth to the ability of intercultural communication. The representation of culture in ELT materials should be organized by taking the current needs of the learners of the 21st century. Three types of cultures have importance for learners because teaching culture is enriching learners and empowering them for their future needs. The way culture is dealt with is of great importance, as well. The cultural elements that enable students to process language acquisition properly should be presented. In this process, all agents of education are vital but coursebooks matter a lot since they carry the objectives of the course and help teachers to follow a syllabus. Thus, the selection of the coursebook should depend on the knowledge provided and suggestions mentioned in the earlier sections.

References

Abdelwahab, M. M. (2013). Developing an English language textbook evaluative checklist. *IOSR Journal of Research & Method in Education*, *1*(3), 55–70.

Alptekin, C. (2002). Towards intercultural communicative competence in ELT. *ELT Journal*, *56*(1), 57–64.

Arslan, S. (2016). An analysis of two Turkish EFL books in terms of cultural aspects. *Procedia - Social and Behavioral Sciences*, *232*(2016), 217 – 225.

Başal, P. (2015). *Investigation of cultural elements in secondary English coursebooks.* Unpublished master's thesis, Yıldız Technical University, Istanbul.

Brown, H. D. (1994). *Principles of language learning and teaching.* Englewood Cliffs, NJ: Prentice Hall Regents.

Byram, M., & Feng, A. (2004). Culture and language learning: Teaching, research and scholarship. *Language teaching, 37*(3), 149–168.

Byrd, P. (2001). Textbooks: Evaluation for selection and analysis for implementation. In M. Celce-Murcia (Ed.), *Teaching English as a second or foreign language* (3rd ed.,, pp. 415–427). Boston, MA: Heinle & Heinle.

Büyükkantarcıoğlu, N. (2004). A sociolinguistic analysis of the present dimension of English as a foreign language in Turkey. *International Journal of Sociology of Languages, 135*(2004), 33–58.

Center for Open Educational Resources & Language Learning, T. (2020). Which culture? | Foreign language teaching methods: Culture. Retrieved 27 March 2020, from https://coerll.utexas.edu/methods/modules/culture/01/which.php.

Cephe, P. T., & Aşık, A. (2016). CEFR and foreign language teaching in Turkey. In İ. Yaman, E. Ekmekçi, & M. Şenel (Eds.), *Current trends in ELT* (pp. 258–269). Ankara: NüansYayıcılık.

Chlopik, Z. (2008). The intercultural approach to EFL teaching and learning. *English Language Forum, 4,* 10–19. Retrieved 25 March 2020, from http://exchanges.state.gov/englishteaching/forum/archives/docs/08-46-4-c.pdf.

Choudhury, M. H. (2013). Teaching culture in EFL: Implications, challenges and strategies. *IOSR Journal of Humanities and Social Science, 13*(1), 20–24.

Cortazzi, M. (2000). *Languages, cultures and cultures of learning in the global classrooms.* Singapore: SEAMEO Regional Language Center.

Cortazzi, M., & Jin, L. (1999). Cultural mirrors: Materials and methods in the EFL classroom. In E. Hinkel (Ed.), *Culture in second language teaching and learning* (pp. 196–219). Cambridge, England: Cambridge University Press.

Cunningsworth, A. (1995). *Choosing your coursebook.* Oxford: Heinemann.

Çakır, I. (2010). The frequency of culture-specific elements in the ELT coursebooks at elementary schools in Turkey. *Novitas-ROYAL (Research on Youth and Language), 4*(2), 182–189.

Çalman, M. (2017). *An evaluation of a course book in the development of intercultural competence.* Unpublished master's thesis, Çağ Üniversitesi, Mersin.

Çavuşer-Özdemir, E., Çavuşer-Yünlü, Z. T., İlter, B., İzgi, İ., & Yeter-Türkeri, A. (2018). *Mastermind.* Ankara: Ministry of National Education.

Çelik, S., & Erbay, Ş. (2013). Cultural perspective of Turkish ELT coursebooks: Do standardized teaching texts incorporate intercultural features? *Education and Science, 38*(167), 336–351.

Daoud, A., & Celce-Murcia, M. (1979). Selecting and evaluating a textbook. In M. Celce-Murcia, & L. McIntosh (Eds.), *Teaching English as a second or foreign language* (pp. 302–307). New York: Newbury House.

Demir, Y., & Ertas, A. (2014). A suggested eclectic checklist for ELT coursebook evaluation. *Reading, 14*(2), 243–252.

Demirbaş, N. (2013). Investigating intercultural elements in English coursebooks. *Kırşehir Eğitim Fakultesi Dergisi (KEFAD), 14*(2), 291–304.

Garinger, D. (2002). Textbook selection for the ESL classroom. ERIC Digest ERO –FL-02-10. Retrieved from: http://www.cal.org/resources/digest/digest_pdfs/0210garinger.pdf.

Ghorbani, M. R. (2011). Quantification and graphic representation of EFL textbook evaluation results. *Theory and Practice in Language Studies, 1*(5), 511–520.

Gómez Rodríguez, L. F. (2015). The cultural content in EFL textbooks and what teachers need to do about it. *PROFILE: Issues in Teachers' Professional Development, 12*(2), 167–187.

Gray, J. (2002). The global coursebook in English language teaching. In D. Block and D. Cameron (Eds.), *Globalization and Language Teaching* (pp. 151–67). London: Routledge.

Gürsoy, E. (2014). Intercultural awareness and its integration to young learner classes: Prospective teachers' views. In P. Romanovski (Ed.), *Intercultural issues in the era of globalization* (pp. 65–74). Warsaw: Wydawnictwo Naukowe Instytutu Komunikacji Specjalistycznej i Interkulturowej Uniwersytet Warszawski.

Halliwell, S. (1992). *Teaching English in the primary classroom.* UK: Longman.

Hinkel, E. (Ed.) (1999). *Culture in second language teaching and learning.* Cambridge: Cambridge University Press.

Işık, A. (2011). Language education and ELT materials in Turkey from the path dependence perspective. *H. U. Journal of Education, 40*(40), 256–266.

Jahan, R., & Roger, P. T. (2006). Global perspectives on the notion of 'target culture' associated with English as a foreign language. *University of Sydney papers in TESOL, 1*(1), 1–17.

Jenkins, J. (2006). Current perspectives on teaching World Englishes and English as a lingua franca. *TESOL Quarterly, 40*(1), 157–181.

Kachru, B. B. (1985). *Standards, codification and sociolinguistic realism: The English language in the outer circle*. na.

Kachru, B. B. (1976). Models of English for the Third World: white man's linguistic burden or language pragmatics? *Tesol Quarterly, 10*(2), 221–239.

Kaldar-Birincioğlu, E., & Karamil, L. (2019). *Relearn!* Ankara, Çankaya: Pasifik Yayınları.

Ke, I. C. (2012). From EFL to English as international and scientific language: Analysing Taiwan's high-school English textbook in the period 1952–2009. *Language, Culture and Curriculum, 25*(2), 173–187.

Kim, S., & Paek, J. (2015). An analysis of culture-related content in English textbooks. *Linguistic Research, 32* (Special Edition), 83–104.

Kırkgöz, Y. (2009). Globalization and English language policy in Turkey. *Educational Policy, 23*(5), 663–684.

Kitao, K. (1991). Teaching culture in foreign language instruction in the United States. *Doshisha Studies in English, 52*(53), 285–306.

Kramsch, C. (1993). *Context and culture in language teaching*. Oxford: Oxford University Press

Kramsch, C. (2013). Culture in foreign language teaching. *Iranian Journal of Language Teaching Research, 1*(1), 57–78.

Kramsch, C., & Widdowson, H. G. (1998). *Language and culture*. Oxford: Oxford University Press.

Kumaravadivelu, B. (2008). Individual identity, cultural globalization and teaching English as an international language: The case of an epistemic break. In L. Alsagoff et al. (Eds.), *Principles and practices for teaching English as an international language* (pp. 9–28). London: Routledge.

Liddicoat, A. J., Papademetre, L., Scarino, A., & Kohler, M. (2003). *Report on intercultural language learning*. Canberra ACT: Commonwealth of Australia.

Liddicoat, A. J., & Scarino, A. (2013). *Intercultural language teaching and learning*. Chichester: Wiley-Blackwell.

Litz, D. R. (2005). Textbook evaluation and ELT management: A South Korean case study. *Asian EFL Journal, 48*(1), 1–53.

Masuhara, H., & Tomlinson, B. (2008). Materials for general English. In . B. Tomlinson (Ed.), *English language learning materials: A critical review* (pp. 17–38). London: Continuum.

McKay, S. L. (2004). Western culture and the teaching of English as an international language. *English Teaching Forum, 42*(2), 10–15.

Nomnian, S. (2013). Thai cultural aspects in English language textbooks in a Thai secondary school. *Veridian E-Journal International, 6*(7), 13–30.

Özcan, E. N. (2019). *The analysis of global values in ELT coursebooks published by the Ministry of National Education for 2018-2019 academic years.* Unpublished master's thesis, Bursa Uludağ Üniversitesi, Bursa.

Peterson, B. (2004). *Cultural intelligence: A guide to working with people from other cultures.* Yarmouth, ME: Intercultural Press.

Razmjoo, S. A. (2010). Developing a textbook evaluation scheme for the expanding circle. *Iranian Journal of Applied Language Studies, 2*(1), 121–136.

Shin, J., Eslami, Z. R., & Chen, W. C. (2011). Presentation of local and international culture in current international English-language teaching textbooks. *Language, Culture and Curriculum, 24*(3), 253–268.

Siddiqie, S. A. (2011). Intercultural exposure through English language teaching: An analysis of an English language textbook in Bangladesh. *Journal of Pan-pacific Association of Applied Linguistics, 15*(2), 109–127.

Silvia, A. (2015). The representation of culture in English textbooks prescribed for high schools in Indonesia. *Indonesian Journal of English Education, 2*(1), 1–16.

Skierso, A. (1991). Textbook selection and evaluation. In M. Celce-Murcia (Ed.), *Teaching English as a second or foreign language* (pp. 432–453). Boston: Heinle and Heinle Publishers.

Sowa, E. (2014). Addressing intercultural awareness-raising in the young learner EFL classroom in Poland: Some teacher perspectives. In *International perspectives on teaching English to young learners* (pp. 104–122). London: Palgrave Macmillan.

Tekir, S., & Arikan, A. (2007). An analysis of English language teaching coursebooks by Turkish writers: "Let's speak English 7" example. *Online Submission, 4*(2), 1–18.

Tıraş, B. (2018). *Upswing English 8 students' book.* Ankara, Keçiören: Tutku Yayıncılık.

Troncoso, C. R. (2010). The effects of language materials on the development of intercultural competence. In . B. Tomlinson & H. Masuhara (Eds.), *Research for materials development in language learning* (pp. 83–103). London: Continuum.

Ulum, Ö. G., & Bada, E. (2016). Cultural elements in EFL course books. *Gaziantep University Journal of Social Sciences, 15*(1), 15–26.

Yaman, İ. (2017). The role of culture in English language teaching. *IX. Uluslararası Eğitim Araştırmaları Birliği Kongresi Eğitim Araştırmaları Birliği, Ordu.*

Yuen, K. M. (2011). The representation of foreign cultures in English textbooks. *ELT Journal*, *65*(4), 458–466.

Williams, D. (1983). Developing criteria for textbook evaluation. *ELT Journal*, *37*(3), 251–255.

Appendix: Suggested Eclectic Coursebook Evaluation Checklist (Demir & Ertaş, 2014, p. 250)

ELT Coursebook Evaluation Checklist		
Subjects & Contents	**Yes**	**No**
Does the content serve as a window into learning about the target language culture (American, British etc.)?		
Are the subject and content of the coursebook interesting?		
Is the content of the coursebook challenging enough to foster new learning?		
Are the subject and content of the coursebook motivating?		
Is the thematic content understandable for students?		
Is there sufficient variety in the subject and content of the coursebook?		
Is the thematic content culturally appropriate?		
Are the topics and texts free from any kind of discrimination (gender, race etc.)?		
Is there a relationship between the content of the coursebook and real-life situations (society)?		
Do the topics and texts in the coursebook include elements from both local and target culture?		
Skills & Sub-skills		
Are there adequate and appropriate exercises and tasks for improving reading comprehension?		
Is there is a wide range of different reading texts with different subject content?		

ELT Coursebook Evaluation Checklist		
Are the reading selections authentic pieces of language?		
Does the coursebook have appropriate listening tasks with well-defined goals?		
Is the listening material well recorded, as authentic as possible?		
Is the listening material accompanied by background information, questions and activities which help comprehension?		
Does the coursebook include speech situations relevant to students' background?		
Are the activities developed to initiate meaningful communication?		
Does the coursebook include adequate individual and group speaking activities?		
Are models provided for different genres?		
Do the tasks have achievable goals and take into consideration learner capabilities?		
Is practice provided in controlled and guided composition in the early stages?		
Does the vocabulary load (i.e. the number of new words introduced every lesson) seem to be reasonable for the students of that level?		
Is there is a good distribution (simple to complex) of vocabulary load across chapters and the whole book?		
Do the vocabulary exercises promote internalization of previously and newly introduced items?		
Are the new vocabulary words repeated in subsequent lessons to reinforce their meaning and use?		
Is the new vocabulary integrated in varying contexts and situations?		
Are the grammar points presented with brief and easy examples and explanations?		

ELT Coursebook Evaluation Checklist		
Is the primary function of new structures for interaction and communication?		
Do the structures gradually increase in complexity to suit the growing reading ability of students?		
Are the new structures presented systematically and in a meaningful context?		
Are the grammar points recycled in the following units?		
Is there sufficient work on recognition and production of stress patterns, intonation and individual sounds?		
Are the pronunciation points repeated and reinforced in subsequent lessons?		
Does the coursebook cover other sub-skills like note-taking, skimming, scanning, inferring meaning, listening for gist, etc.?		
Layout & Physical Make-up		
Is the printing quality high?		
Does the coursebook look interesting and fun?		
Does the coursebook include a detailed overview of the functions and structures that will be taught in each unit?		
Does the coursebook reflect learners' preferences in terms of layout, design, and organization?		
Does the coursebook contain enough pictures, diagrams, tables etc. helping students understand the printed text?		
Are the illustrations informative and functional?		
Do the size and weight of the coursebook seem convenient for students to handle?		
Practical Considerations		
Is the coursebook up-to-date (e.g. published within the past 10 years)?		
Is the coursebook easily accessible?		
Is the coursebook affordable?		

ELT Coursebook Evaluation Checklist		
Does the coursebook have supplementary materials (tapes, visuals etc.)?		
Does the coursebook have supporting online materials/tests and e-format?		
Does the book address different learning styles and strategies?		
Do the activities and exercises introduce the main principles of CLT?		
Does the coursebook include self-assessment parts?		
Can the activities be exploited fully and embrace various methodologies in ELT?		
Is/are the type/s of syllabus design used in the book appropriate for learners?		
Can the coursebook easily be integrated into technology, thereby allowing for individual study outside the school?		
Does the coursebook fit curriculum/goals?		
Are the objectives specified explicitly in the coursebook?		
Is the coursebook designed by taking into account the learners' socially and historically English-free status?		
EXTRA COMMENTS/CRITICISMS ON THE BOOK		
*According to Ersoz (n.d.), if the number of YES answers is more than 80 %, the book is perfect for your situation. If between 60–80 %, it can be used in your situation but needs adaptation. If below 60 %, the book is not suitable for your situation.		

Mehmet Galip Zorba and Arda Arikan

4 Developing Intercultural Communicative Competence through Literature

Introduction

The 21st century refers to a globalizing world in which various identities and tangible lines separating nations and peoples move continuously as cultures merge. This new phase of human history can be felt in the case of Turkey where millions of Syrian, Afghani, Georgian, Central Asian, and Russian migrants have settled down with various hopes.

Research in education has articulated that "One way to equip our students with the linguistic and cultural skills to communicate successfully with people from diverse backgrounds is to foster their development of intercultural competence" (Schenker, 2012, p. 449). Although acquiring or learning a foreign language helps members of culturally or linguistically different groups communicate, "being proficient in a foreign language does not guarantee successful communication with people from diverse cultural backgrounds" (Schenker, 2012, p. 450).

History of foreign language teaching in relation to the teaching of culture is proposed by Risager (2007) suggests that the major breakthrough that brought the issue into consideration started in 1950s with the works of Lado and Brooks among others. In 1970s, the issue was framed within the binary opposition of the native and non-native cultures whereas in 1980s, the pendulum moved towards a rather more dynamic understanding of culture in foreign language teaching followed by the effects of globalization which gained fervent discussion in 1990s. Since then, we can easily say that culture has still been considered as an important issue in foreign language teaching regardless of the various aspects attached to it ranging from methods and instructional activities to assessment and identity issues including conflict resolution and peace education among many others. At present, culture and foreign language learning and teaching is in constant influx and formation depending on the context, theoretical lenses of the researchers, and the instructional methods employed all of which produce a variety and often conflicting messages about this relationship come to the surface and flourish in numerous ways. As Risager (2006) articulates in another study, in such a realm, a Danish woman learning Turkish in Denmark as a part of her daily interaction

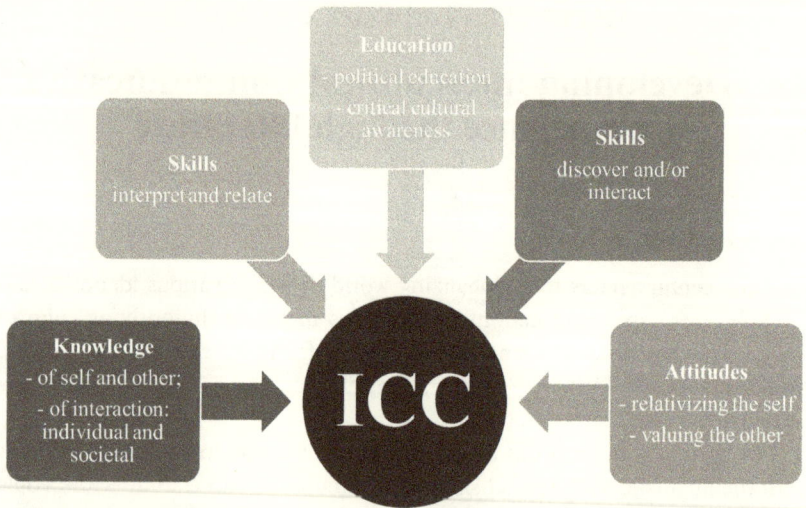

Fig. 1: Components of Byram's Model of Intercultural Communicative Competence (ICC) (adapted from Byram, 1997, p. 34)

with her Turkish husband should be considered as learning a foreign language as a second language, which suggests that our previous understandings and ways of seeing have been challenged in the globalizing world.

Research has produced a bulk of models theorizing ICC within the context of foreign language education. Among many, Byram's (1997) model of intercultural communicative competence is composed of five major objectives that learners must retain in order to become competent communicators from an intercultural perspective. The five objectives proposed include attaining knowledge of self and other, developing attitudes of openness and curiosity, gaining skills of interpreting and relating and skills of discovery and interaction, and obtaining critical cultural awareness (Schenker, 2012, p. 450).

Culture and Literature Relationship

Although there are numerous definitions of culture, in foreign language teaching, culture is often defined in a way to include all material and conceptual properties of a specific group of people. This working definition is comprehensive enough as far as educational sciences and practices are concerned for as it incorporates both physical (concrete and visible) as well as ideological (invisible) entities.

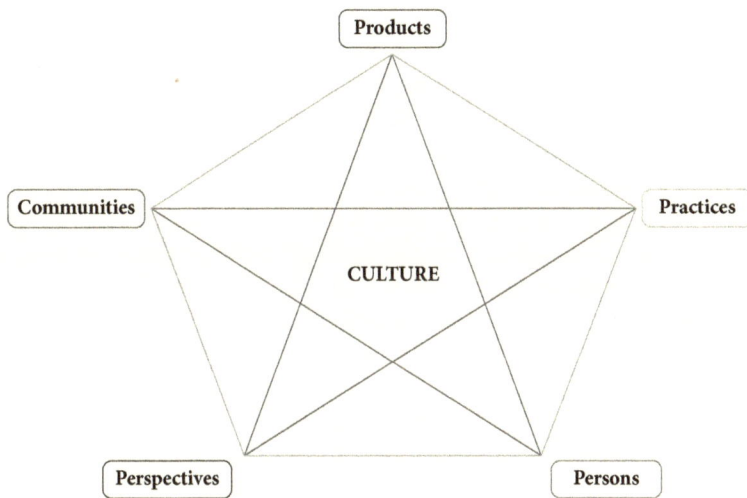

Fig. 2: Five Dimensions of Culture (adapted from Moran, 2001, p. 24)

Moran's (2001) definition of culture is based on such a distinction between tangible and intangible cultural elements and elaborately divides culture into five dimensions (see Fig. 1).

Moran (2001) defines culture as "a complex and multi-layered system that portrays the evolving way of life of a group of persons, consisting of a shared set of practices associated with a shared set of products, based upon a shared set of perspectives on the world, and set within specific social contexts" (Moran, 2001, pp. 24–25). Accordingly, as shown in Fig. 2, each dimension depends on and is interrelated with the others. This model is also useful to show the complicated nature of culture. In such an intertwined and multifaceted cultural model, explaining the relationship between culture and literature is not a simple task.

Echoing the complex relationship between culture and literature, Valdes (2001) demystifies that literature is certainly culture in action, yet it is much more than that because its major function is not to serve as a medium to transmit the culture of the people who speak the language (p. 137). Lazar (2005) accentuates the fictional nature of literary works and points out that they are not factual documents, thus what aspects of a given culture are portrayed and how reliably they are presented are still important questions (p. 16). Nevertheless, literary works are among the precious artifacts of the "Big C" culture of a given society which refers to most visible cultural products

(Tomalin & Stempleski, 1993). In a similar vein, in Moran's (2001) cultural model, it is obvious that literary works fall into the dimension of cultural products at the surface level. Although they are one of the most valuable cultural artifacts, their contents often function as authentic materials in foreign language classrooms. From this stance, contents of literary works provide various examples of linguistic practices of a given culture, showing the real use of the language. In a similar vein, as McKay (2001) underlines, literary works are useful tools to show how a language is used in the aesthetic, sociological, pragmatic and sociolinguistic senses in life-like contexts. Besides, Kramsch (1993) also adds that literary works present everyday language along with the ways to how break with it. Furthermore, although the "world" created in many literary works are fictional, their contents still offer thorough contexts in which the way of life of culturally different people is vividly portrayed, which can give students "a feel for the codes and preoccupations that structure a real society" (Collie & Slater, 2006, p. 4). Such colorfully described contexts involve various culturally rich snapshots picturing frames of cultural practices, perspectives, persons and communities. Accordingly, literary works also function as opening windows to the culture of the people whose language is studied (Lazar, 2005, p. 16) and thus foster cultural enrichment in the classroom. Moreover, literary texts exemplify many social, political and/or historical events that have shaped a given culture or society (Collie & Slater, 2006). Such events are sometimes directly portrayed as the story is based on them or they are employed as embellishments to form a background for the storyline. In both cases, interpretation of such texts can also lead students to gain deeper insights and understandings of social, political and historical milestones (Hall, 2005; Topuzova, 2001).

Intercultural Communicative Competence and Literary Texts

Seelye (1993) underlines that the power of literary works to understand another culture relies heavily on the nature of literature as the ability to enter a literary world is similar to the ability to enter in another culture because, in both cases, people suspend "usual" conventions to accept a different set of premises (p. 70).

As Byram (1997) postulates, literary texts are useful authentic materials for developing intercultural communicative competence as documents and cultural products generated by culturally different social groups help students to know about and appreciate events, thoughts, and national memories of a culture.

Ghosn (2002) argues that "Literature can also act as a powerful change agent by developing pupils' intercultural awareness while at the same time nurturing empathy, a tolerance for diversity, and emotional intelligence" (p. 172). In such development, "However, if children learning a foreign language are to gain insight into the target language culture, they should read high quality contemporary fiction which shows the characters in contexts that accurately reflect the culture of the English-speaking world today" (p. 177). Hence, although any literary text can be read for pleasure, literary texts that are thought to develop students' ICC must be chosen carefully.

Intercultural Competence and Language Classrooms

According to Zacharias (2005), a review of literature on the learning of culture learning may include:

1. Cultural problem solving
2. Contrasting and comparing cultures
3. Role plays
4. Value hierarchies.

Cultural problem solving can be framed in a way to present a real-life cultural problem in the classroom and then asking students to suggest ways to overcome this troublesome situation. A comparison of cultures can be made by delivering a theme or practice and then asking students to collect data on how this theme or practice is experienced in at least two different cultures. For example, asking students to compare how marriage expenditure is dealt in different cultures can be an example to this activity.

Gómez (2012) argues that "The Common European Framework of References to Languages (Council of Europe, 2001) also points out the role played by literature in EFL as a potential means to develop language and interculturality: Imaginative and artistic uses of language are important both educationally and in their own right" (p. 52). Although almost all activities and tasks can be used to foster students' openness towards tolerance for diversity, reading, writing, discussions and role plays are known to be the most applicable ones in language classrooms. Role plays are important for students especially when communication is considered. Picking up different characters as their own, students may put themselves in the shoes of others and write scenarios including various cultural issues. While one student may act as the father of the bride, the other may pick up the role of the father of the other to solve a problem such as dealing with the expenditures. As students will come to understand, part of the problem with ICC is that values and how values are prioritized differ from one person or community to another. Thus, asking students to collect how members of their own culture and others' prioritize certain cultures aspects, preferably by preparing lists in order of importance, is a great way to engage students in understanding how individuals ascribe different levels of importance to values.

Gómez (2012) uses John Steinbeck's famous short story titled "The Chrysanthemums" which portrays the daily routine of a married couple living on a farm. To develop his students' understanding of others, he asks the following questions (p. 64):

1. In the description of the setting, Steinbeck remarks that the fog "sat like a lid on the mountains and made of the great valley a closed pot". Moreover, it is December with "pale cold sunshine". Later, he describes Elisa enclosed in her garden working eagerly, and the garden is surrounded by a "wire fence". How does the setting affect Elisa's life? What is the meaning of the environment in relation to Elisa' daily life?
2. Compare Elisa's activities on the farm to those of her husband's. What can you say about the issue of gender? Do they do the same activities, and do they have the same opportunities?
3. Based on your reading, are Elisa and Henry a happily married couple? Support your answer.
4. Study the conversation between Elisa and the tinker. What is his real intention when he comes to Elisa's farm? What kind of a man is he? Does he want to establish a friendly relationship with Elisa?
5. What are the similarities and differences between Elisa's husband and the tinker? How do they affect or favor Elisa?
6. Is Elisa sympathetic or unsympathetic to the tinker? Why does she please the tinker with everything he asks for (the chrysanthemum sprouts, the flowerpot, and the saucepans to be repaired)?
7. Does Elisa change physically and emotionally throughout the whole story? If so, how and why does she change? What theme or idea do you think Steinbeck intends to show through her change?

With the help of these comprehension, reflection and discussion questions, as Gómez (2012) states, "Learners can manipulate information, express personal ideas, compare and contrast information, find and investigate historical events and literary topics, defend a point of view, and address conclusions from the literary works they read" (p. 61). Thus, depending on the content of the literary text selected for reading, students will prepare personal projects to discover not only other cultures, but also other lives. By doing this, they will come to see that cultures are interwoven in our daily lives, that is, it does not have to be

Tab. 1: Activities, Objectives, and Products for ICC

Activities	Objectives	Products
1 Reading for information and note-taking	• Raising curiosity • Learning knowledge about other cultures and individuals	• Finding specific information about Chicanas (Mexican-Americans) and writing notes • Learning about Sandra Cisneros and taking notes
2 Writing	• Taking a model (Cisneros' text) and writing a similar one from real-life • Interpreting and relating others' lives with one's own	Comparing and contrasting culturally unique behaviors and beliefs
3 Poster preparation	Evaluating different perspectives	A poster showing student's perception of his family and friends' hair
4 Reading and writing for values	Identifying and interpreting explicit and implicit values in texts	Students chose another chapter from the text and jot down some values they attain from the text

something distinguishable such as a specific folk dance or a practice, but what we do daily.

Another example to using literary texts for ICC purposes can be drawn from Sandra Cisneros' (1984) book titled *The House on Mango Street* whose narrator, Esperanza, is a small child of Chicano (Mexican American) origin. This short chapter titled "Hairs" is as follows:

Everybody in our family has different hair. My Papa's hair is like a broom, all up in the air. And me, my hair is lazy. It never obeys barrettes or bands. Carlos' hair is thick and straight. He doesn't need to comb it. Nenny's hair is slippery-slides out of your hand. And Kiki, who is the youngest, has hair like fur.

But my mother's hair, my mother's hair, like little \ rosettes, like little candy circles all curly and pretty because she pinned it in pincurls all day, sweet to put your nose J into when she is holding you, holding you and you feel safe, is the warm smell of bread before you bake it, is the smell when she makes room for you on her side of the bed still warm with her skin, and you sleep near her, the rain outside falling and Papa snoring. The snoring, the rain, and Mama's hair that smells like bread.

In Tab. 1, a sample of activities are given to exemplify how *The House on Mango Street* as a literary text can be used for ICC purposes.

Tab. 2: Objectives of Intercultural Communicative Competence for Teaching, Learning and Assessment (adapted from Byram, 1997, pp. 57–64).

Components	Descriptions
Attitudes	curiosity and openness, readiness to suspend disbelief about other cultures and belief about one's own
Knowledge	of social groups and their products and practices in one's own and in one's interlocutor's country, and of the general processes of societal and individual interaction
Skills of interpreting and relating	ability to interpret a document or event from another culture, to explain it and relate it to documents or events from one's own
Skills of discovery and interaction	ability to acquire new knowledge of a cul of a culture and cultural practices and the ability to operate , attitudes and skills under the constraints of real-time communication and interaction
Critical cultural awareness/political education	ability to evaluate, critically and based on explicit criteria, perspectives, practices and products in one's own and other cultures and countries

Assessing ICC through Teaching of Literature

Assessing intercultural communicative competence can be challenging and complicated for many teachers as assessment is directly related to learning objectives and/or gains. In other words, these objectives or gains can be regarded as guidelines for what to assess. Holding this view, Byram (1997) proposes a set of objectives of intercultural communicative competence to be used for teaching, learning and assessment, and these objectives are also categorized in five different components as shown in the table given below.

As can be seen in Tab. 2 given above, each component is described with a set of keywords which also limit the scope of each component. Accordingly, teachers can use these descriptions as objectives and/or gains while designing a lesson or an assessment tool. Furthermore, teachers can also elaborate these descriptors, specifying them according to their or students' needs (see Tab. 3).

It should be noted that some the specific objectives given in Tab. 3 still require more elaboration so that they can function assessment objectives (or lesson objectives), which makes assessing intercultural communicative competence demanding and challenging for many teachers. In addition to caveat, it is also demanding to find an appropriate literary text and converting it to an assessment tool. Therefore, a sample is provided to show how to elaborate such objectives (see Tab. 4).

Tab. 3: Specific Objectives for The Components of Intercultural Communicative Competence (adapted from Byram, 1997, pp. 57–64).

Components	Specific Objectives
Attitudes	• willingness to question the values and presuppositions in cultural practices and products in one's own environment • readiness to engage with the conventions and rites of verbal and non-verbal communication and interaction.
Knowledge	• historical and contemporary relationships between one's own and one's interlocutor's countries • the types of cause and process of misunderstanding between interlocutors of different cultural origins.
Skills of interpreting and relating	• identifying ethnocentric perspectives in a document or event and explain their origins. • mediating between conflicting interpretations of phenomena
Skills of discovery and interaction	• identifying significant references within and across cultures and elicit their significance • identifying similar and dissimilar processes of interaction, verbal and non-verbal, and negotiating an appropriate use of them in specific circumstances
Critical cultural awareness/political education	identifying and interpreting explicit and implicit values in documents and events in one's own and other cultures making an evaluative analysis of the documents and events which refers to an explicit perspective and criteria

In order to assess the objectives given above various assessment techniques can be used, yet it should be underlined that assessment of intercultural communicative competence should be more formative and continuous rather than summative and being fixed-point (Lussier et al., 2007, pp. 29–30) because formative assessment requires "an ongoing process of gathering information on the extent of learning and on strengths and weaknesses" (CoE, 2001, p. 186) whereas continuous assessment focuses on "class performances, pieces of work and projects throughout the course, and thus the final grade reflects the whole course, semester or year". (CoE, 2001, p. 185). Lussier et al. (2007) also suggest various assessment techniques ranging from self-evaluation, culture-logs, portfolios, surveys to tasks mainly focusing on comparisons, explanations, analyses and descriptions.

The assessment framework of intercultural communicative competence suits well to the Turkish context as the assessment aspect of the national English language teaching curricula involves a blend of "alternative and process-oriented testing procedures" with traditional assessment tools for assessing production of language

Tab. 4: Sample for Generating Specific Lesson/Assessment Objectives of Intercultural Communicative Competence

Components	Specific Objectives	Assessment Objectives
1 Skills of discovery and interaction	Identifying similar and dissimilar processes of interaction, verbal and non-verbal	Finding specific information about how culturally different people verbally and non-verbally greet in an excerpt taken from a literary work
2 Critical cultural awareness/political education	Identifying and interpreting explicit and implicit values in documents and events in one's own and other cultures	Comparing and contrasting culturally unique behaviors of politeness and the reasons behind them through short series of simple phrases and sentences linked into a list

(MoNE, 2018, p. 6). Such a wide scope of assessment provides a plethora of assessment techniques for each language skills, and some of them are given in Tab. 5.

In a nutshell, assessing intercultural communicative competence requires setting appropriate objectives, using various assessment techniques and it should not be restricted to employing summative and fixed-point assessment. Considering doing all these by using literary works, these may seem an extra heavy burden on teachers. However, it should be underlined that teachers still have the most important role in actualizing teaching of all those written plans and objectives in the classroom and assessing students' competence. Accordingly, no matter how demanding and time-consuming it is, assessing intercultural communicative competence is not beyond the skill of a well-organized teacher.

Conclusion

In conclusion, today's world necessitates using the English language in multicultural and multilingual settings as a medium of communication. In such culturally and linguistically diverse settings, students will need to perform more than communicative competence to engage in today's world as competent communicators. Intercultural communicative competence is suggested to fill this gap. Various models have been proposed and various ways have been so far suggested to improve intercultural communicative competence. Considering the relationship between literature and culture and what literary works offer for better English language learning, using literary works to develop intercultural communicative competence seems theoretically reasonable and methodologically viable.

Tab. 5: Skills and Assessment Techniques (adapted from MoNE, 2018, p. 8)

Skill	Assessment Techniques
Speaking	• Collaborative or singular drama performances (simulations, role-plays, side-coaching) • Group or pair discussions • Describing a picture/video/story, etc. • Discussing a picture/video/story, etc.
Listening	• Identifying interlocutors' intentions and implicatures • Listening and perform/complete an action • Understanding overall meaning and supporting details • Recognizing specific information
Reading	• Finding specific information, identifying the gist and supporting details • Read and perform/complete and action • Transferring the text to a table/chart (information transfer) • Understanding the author's intention
Writing	• Describing a picture/visual/video, etc. • Filling in a form • Reporting a table or a chart, • Rephrasing • Rewriting

References

Byram, M. (1997). *Teaching and assessing intercultural communicative competence*. Clevedon, UK: Multilingual Matters.

Cisneros, S. (1984). *The house on Mango street*. New York: Vintage Contemporaries.

Collie, J., & Slater, S. (2006). *Literature in the language classroom: A resource book of ideas and activities*. Cambridge: Cambridge University Press.

Council of Europe. (2001). *Common European framework of reference for languages: Learning, teaching, assessment*. Strasbourg: Council of Europe.

Ghosn, I. K. (2002). Four good reasons to use literature in primary school ELT. *ELT Journal, 56*(2), 172–179.

Gómez, L. F. (2012). Fostering intercultural communicative competence through reading authentic literary texts in an advanced Colombian EFL classroom: A constructivist perspective. *Profile, 14*, 1, 49–66.

Hall, G. (2005). *Literature in language education*. New York: Palgrave Macmillan.

Kramsch, C. (1993). *Context and culture in language teaching*. Oxford. Oxford University Press.

Lazar, G. (2005). *Literature and language teaching: A guide for teachers and trainers.* Cambridge: Cambridge University Press.

Lussier, D., Golubina, K., Ivanus, D., Kostova, S. C., Retamar, G., M., Skopinskaja, L., & Wiesinger, S. (2007). Guidelines for the assessment of intercultural communicative competence (ICC). In I. Lázár, M. Huber-Kriegler, D. Lussier, G. S. Matei, & C. Peck (Eds.), *Developing and assessing intercultural communicative competence: A guide for language teachers and teacher educators* (pp. 23–40). Strasbourg: Council of Europe.

McKay, S. L. (2001). Literature as content for ESL/EFL. In M. Celce-Murcia (Ed.), *Teaching English as second or foreign language* (pp. 319–332). Boston: Heinle, Cengage Learning.

Ministry of National Education. (2017). *English language curriculum for primary and secondary education (grades 2, 3, 4, 5, 6, 7 and 8).* Ankara. MEB.

Moran, P. R. (2001). *Teaching culture.* Boston: Heinle, Cengage Learning.

Schenker, T. (2012). Intercultural competence and cultural learning through telecollaboration. *CALICO Journal, 29*(3), 449–470.

Seelye, H. N. (1993). *Teaching culture: Strategies for intercultural communication.* Chicago: National Textbook Company.

Tomalin, B., & Stempleski, S. (1993). *Cultural awareness.* Oxford: Oxford University Press.

Topuzova, K. (2001). British and Bulgarian Christmas cards: A research project for students. In M. Byram, A. Nichols, & D. Stevens (Eds.), *Developing intercultural competence in practice* (pp. 246–259). Clevedon, UK: Multilingual Matters.

Valdes, J. M. (2001). Culture in literature. In J. M. Valdes (Ed.), *Culture Bound: Bridging the cultural gap in language teaching* (pp. 137–147). Cambridge: Cambridge University Press.

Zacharias, N. T. (2005). Developing intercultural competence through literature. *CELT, 5*(1), 27–41.

Berna Güryay

5 Developing Intercultural Competence through Creative Drama

Introduction

> Creative drama in its truest and deepest sense cannot be stereotyped.
> It's like a river- always on the move-making connections:
> Connecting river banks,
> Connecting starting points and destinations;
> Connecting through improvisation,
> Action and reaction,
> Initiative and response,
> Thinking and feeling;
> Relations between people, ideas, even centuries!
>
> (Julie Thompson cited in McCaslin, 1990:2)

As Julie Thompson (Former director of Children's Centre for the Creative Arts) states above, creative drama is a way to connect people's varying ideas and attitudes. Increasing the emphatic skills of the target group is one of the clearest reasons for using creative drama. Empathy is also a key factor for developing "intercultural competence", defined as a combination of attitudes, knowledge, understanding and skills applied through action, which supports respect for cultural differences and allows effective communication across cultures (Huber & Reynolds, 2014). Drama enables humans to confront situations which involve significant change, preparing them to deal with those challenges when they arise (Heathcote, 1991). Consequently, creative drama can help learners to practice real life situations, i.e., it is the rehearsal for life (Adıgüzel, 2010; Güryay, 2012) and it can give learners insights into multicultural life. In addition, creative drama, more than any other subject in the curriculum, mirrors life as it is lived and experienced; namely, language can be experienced –heard, interpreted and used – in realistic contexts (Winston, 2004). Language learners need not only knowledge and skill in the grammar of a language, but also the ability to use the language in socially and culturally appropriate ways; therefore, language learners who become "intercultural speakers" are likely to be successful both in communicating information and in developing relationship with people of other languages and cultures (Byram, Gribkova, & Starkey, 2002). Creative drama will be an invaluable tool in simultaneously developing learners' language skills and intercultural skills. Briefly, this type of drama is an excellent way to develop intercultural competence and introduce a wide range of cultural diversity. This chapter, after sketching the relationship between creative drama and intercultural competence, aims at explaining the ways of developing intercultural competence in classrooms via creative drama.

Intercultural Competence

In 21st century, people from various countries with different backgrounds are living in close proximity. The picture below from my daughter's nursery classroom in Britain, shows the great diversity in the origin of the students' families, even in a small class. But even where students are still living in their country of origin, diverse groups are able to communicate because of technological developments. In the interstices of the native and target cultures, students are constantly engaged in creating a culture of "the third kind" through the give and take of classroom dialogue (Kramsch, 1993). This multicultural situation should be seen as enriching, and all education systems should develop such intercultural competence.

What Is Intercultural Competence?

Intercultural competence is a combination of attitudes, knowledge, understanding and skills applied through action, which enables people, either alone or together with others, to:

- understand and respect others who are perceived to have different cultural affiliations
- respond appropriately, effectively and respectfully when interacting and communicating with people who are culturally different
- establish positive and constructive relationships with them
- understand oneself and one's own multiple cultural affiliations through encounters with cultural 'difference'.

(Huber& Reynolds, 2014)

Picture 1: The map showing the different countries from which the students' families came to Great Britain (2014)

Creative Drama

What Is Creative Drama?

The word 'drama' originates Thracian city in Greece, characterized as a place by a hill with many water springs. This meaning of drama is related to the action of an object, which can change according to the place or action over time (Adıgüzel, 2006). Drama involves all kinds of actions which contain dramatic moments, and drama emerges as a result of interaction between people, and others, or between people and objects (Adıgüzel, 2010). "Creative drama", in other words, "Drama in Education" or alternatively, "Educational Drama" highlight the educational aspects, developing the cognitive, affective and motional learning (Adıgüzel, 2010). Creative drama shares with all other drama this aspect of change and development. According to the Children's Theatre Association (cited in McCaslin, 1990, p. 5) "Creative drama is an improvisational, nonexhibitional, process-centred, form of drama in which participants are guided by a leader to imagine, enact, and reflect upon human experiences".

The Stages of Creative Drama

San (2006) describes five stages in creative drama; warm-up, sketches, improvisation, formation, and evaluation. However, a study carried out by Adıgüzel (2002, 2006) suggested that these five stages were confusing, and in a later study, based on creative drama experiences, Adıgüzel (2010) proposed just three different stages of creative drama;

1. Warm-up, preparation:
2. Enactment
3. Evaluation-discussion

Preparation-Warming Up

Creative drama can be used in any classroom, but it is difficult to start role playing and improvisation with participants who have never experienced this kind of active participation. Therefore, it is important that creative drama activities begin with preparation and warm-up (Bushman, 2001).

- Preparation-warm up is a stage in which all senses are used simultaneously; it consists introverted exercises, mostly physical activities. Its aim is to establish group dynamics, self-confidence and adaptation and the ultimate goal is to prepare the participants for the following stages (Adıgüzel, 2006).

The procedure of preparation-warm-up stage is much more definite, and the leader is more involved compared to other stages. The plays in this stage ensures that ice is broken between the leader and the participants through enjoyable activities.

In the groups who have recently begun creative drama, the leader should actively participate in the warm-up activities to reduce participants' feelings of embarrassment. The leader's participation helps to lower anxiety levels and motivates the participants.

Enactment

Enactment is a stage during the process where a theme is chosen, developed, and detailed. From an initial starting point, the participants develop the theme through improvisation, role-play and other techniques, either individually or in groups. All experiences, sharing and evaluation in creative drama result directly from the animations done during this stage. The subject of the action generally involves a dramatic moment (Adıgüzel, 2006, 2010). This moment is evaluated in the light of the components of dramatic fiction; roles, dramatic tension, focus, location, time, language, motion, atmosphere, symbols and dramatic meaning (Adıgüzel, 2010).

Evaluation-Discussion

Participants share their feelings and thoughts related to the process at this stage: the essence, importance, qualitative and quantitative dimensions of the process. They also discuss educational attainments, the subject matter and the knowledge. Alternative procedures at this stage are writing in role (for instance, two participants talking about the creative drama process in improvisations) and writing outside role (writing letter, diary, preparing a newspaper article). In this way, the leader gets indirect feedback from the participants. If creative drama is used as a specific educational method, other evaluation techniques can also be employed, such as exams, and attitude scales (Adıgüzel, 2006, 2010).

Creative Drama Techniques

Creative drama makes use of several drama techniques, particularly in the enactment stage. Creative drama teachers should select the appropriate technique for the aims of the lesson. Some of these are explained below.

1. *Improvisation*: Students enact extemporaneously and spontaneously on the theme of a given subject or an object. Variables such as "who, what, where, with whom" shape the improvisation (Ataman, 2009). Creative drama is synonymous with improvisation. All creative drama techniques are different kinds of improvisation (Adıgüzel, 2010).
2. *Role Playing*: The enactment of an idea, a case, a problem or a situation by a group (Adıgüzel, 2006). Role playing students reflects their opinions much more easily in the role of a fictitious character (Adıgüzel, Üstündağ, & Öztürk, 2007). Furthermore, the character research preparation will affect the overall language used and the functional strategies employed during the performance, which in turn, will enable students to communicate on a broad range of topics, creating a context which is as authentic as it is possible to be in the classroom context (DiNapoli, 2003).

3. *Role-Reversal*: Roles can be reversed at individual or group level. As a result, they not only explore demands presented by a future situation, but also reflect on problems and possible solutions (Neelands & Goode, 2010). Furthermore, this technique can be helpful in developing empathy.

4. *Small-group Improvisation-Role Playing*: Small groups plan, prepare and present improvisations as a means of representing a hypothesis, or to demonstrate alternative views/courses of action (Neelands & Goode, 2010).

5. *Whole-group Improvisation-Role Playing*: All students and their teacher participate in the enactment at the same time, to minimize anxiety caused by being watched by others (Adıgüzel, 2010).

6. *Dramatization*: Transforming a story into a play by conveying text's intentions and feelings with movement, voice, gestures and words (Kavcar, 2006).

7. *Teacher in Role*: Teacher adopts a suitable role, and manages the learning opportunities provided by the dramatic context (Neelands & Goode, 2010). Heathcote states that this is an effective technique in groups new to drama (Adıgüzel, 2010).

8. *Flashback*: "Scenes are created which predate an important moment in the drama so that images from the past help explicate or reinforce the relationship between the dramatic present moment and its history" (Neelands & Goode 2010, p. 56).

9. *Interview-conversation-interrogation-discussion*: Based on creating different situations through questions in order to develop emerging knowledge, attitudes, behaviours and talents in drama (Adıgüzel, Üstündağ, & Öztürk, 2007).

10. *Hot-seating*: The protagonist or another important character is seated in front of other group members, and answers questions related to the background, values, behaviours, motives, relationships of the character played. This can also be done with more than one character. The aim is to understand the character/s, and sometimes, to make additions to the story. (Adıgüzel, 2010; Adıgüzel, Üstündağ, & Öztürk, 2007).

11. *Voices in the Head (Conscience Alley)*: The protagonist walks slowly in an alley formed by other group members. The character/s expresses some ideas possibly discordant with those of the protagonist, or acts as the conflicting element in a collective conscience (Adıgüzel, 2010; Neelands & Goode, 2010).

12. *Still-Image*: Groups use their own bodies to create an image to clarifying the meaning of a moment, idea or theme. Alternatively, an individual strikes a pose as a sculpture (Neelands & Goode, 2010).

13. *Group Sculpture*: A student arranges the positions of a small group or to the whole group to achieve a particular objective (Adıgüzel, 2010).

14. *Gossip Circle*: Participants criticize the behaviors of the characters in a crea-
    tive drama process in the form of gossip, which becomes increasingly exag-
    gerated (Adıgüzel, Üstündağ, & Öztürk, 2007).
15. *Writing in Role*: Participants write diaries, letters, journals or messages in
    the role of any character during enactment. This is especially helpful in pre-
    paring children for reading literary texts (Adıgüzel, 2010).
16. *Inner-Voice*: Group members reflect their ideas and feelings about their
    principal values in order to overcome the complexity of the protagonist's
    problem (Adıgüzel, 2010).
17. *Meetings*: The students gather together as part of the drama to discuss new
    information, plan action, make collective decisions and suggest strategies to
    solve problems that have arisen (Neelands & Goode, 2010).
18. *Pantomime*: This is expression of feelings and thoughts without words, using
    only body language (Yılmaz, 2010). "Children enjoy pantomime, and for the
    young child it is an excellent way to begin creative drama" (McCaslin, 1990,
    p. 71).
19. *Role cards*: Role cards give information about the details of the characters.
    Characters do not see his/her partner's role card (Adıgüzel, Üstündağ, &
    Öztürk, 2007).
20. *Rituals, Ceremonies*: Groups devise special events to mark, commemorate or
    celebrate an event or occasion of cultural/historical significance (Neelands
    & Goode, 2010).
21. *Telephone/radio conversations*: A dramatic moment and either good or bad
    news related to this is described in telephone conversations. This news may
    be the starting point of drama, or may develop, direct, formulate or end the
    dramatic situation (Adıgüzel, 2010).
22. *Moment of truth*: This is a means of resolving a drama, with reflective discus-
    sion on the events aimed at predicting the final scene Volunteers act out this
    key moment of tension until the group is satisfied that the moment is true to
    life? (Neelands & Goode, 2010).
23. *Split Screen*: Students prepare two or more stages, which represent different
    times and places. Students can decide to move forward or backwards in
    time, as in a movie (Somers 1994 cited in Adıgüzel, 2010).
24. *Forum Theatre*: A small group enacts a situation while the others observe.
    Observers may take over roles or add new ones at any time (Neelands &
    Goode, 2010). While this is a kind of theatre, it deals with social matters,
    suggests solutions to problems, and involves the audience in the process,
    thus is also a creative drama technique (Adıgüzel, Üstündağ, & Öztürk,
    2007). For Augusto Boal "forum theatre enables children to explore real

life situations with a degree of distance through the creation of fictional characters" (cited in Jindal-Snape et al., 2011).

25. *Space Between*: "Students arrange volunteers from the group, representing characters from the drama, so that the space between them symbolizes how close their relationships currently are" (Neelands & Goode, 2010, p. 86).

26. *Mantle of the Expert*: the group members become characters with specialist knowledge relevant to the situation, such as doctors, historians, social workers (Neelands & Goode, 2010).

27. *Role-on-the-Wall*: the protagonist is drawn on the wall or on the floor and the students add new points via drawing and writing throughout the lesson, (Adıgüzel, 2010).

28. *Walls Have Ears*: "The group make the four walls of a room by standing in lines around a previously crafted still-image of the protagonist. They then collectively reflect back impressions of the key events that have befallen that character through snatches and repetition of dialogue." (Neelands & Goode, 2010, p. 93)

29. *Thought-Tracking*: Private thoughts of the characters are publicly revealed. Students may be frozen in a body position of their own choosing. As soon as the teacher indicates a student, s/he reflects her/his feelings and thoughts (Adıgüzel, 2010).

30. *A Day in the Life*: A large sheet of paper is divided into five, quarters with a circle in the center. In the center, the name and age of a character are written. In the four other sections, students fill in information about the character's "home, family, play, and day". The class is subdivided into four groups, each of which takes a different section and creates a short dialogue between the protagonist and one another character based on the information (Neelands & Goode, 2010).

Why Is Creative Drama Important?

"Education is not the filling of a pail but the lighting of a fire!" says Sir Butler Yeats. Teachers should spark students by motivating and inspiring them rather than spoon-feeding information and lecturing. Only in this way can students become curious, avid and creative learners. In this sense, creative drama can be an effective and alternative method in classrooms because it is student-centered, experiential and communicative.

According to McCaslin (1990: 4) modern education and creative drama share many objectives, such as:

- Creativity and aesthetic development
- The ability to think critically
- Social growth and the ability to work cooperatively with others
- Improved communication skills
- The development of moral and spiritual values
- Knowledge of self

Heathcote (1991) acknowledges that educational drama has two aims, which are both important in personal development: "creative work", and "coping work". Dramatic activity is the result of the ability to role-play – to discover how it feels to be in someone else's shoes. In this way, the participant will identify with others, and re-live or pre-live important situations.

Adıgüzel (2010) suggests some fundamental objectives of creative drama, as follows:

- Development of creativity and imagination
- Development of self-knowledge, self-realization and communication skills
- Development of democratic attitudes and behaviors
- Development of aesthetic behaviors
- Development of critical and independent thinking
- Development of cooperative working
- Creating social sensibility
- The discharge and control of feelings
- Development of language, both verbal and non-verbal expression

In an experiential qualitative study, Laakso (1996) formed a picture of what prospective teachers experienced in educational drama, in other words, creative drama. The findings were encouraging. Interest in creative drama was maintained throughout the knowledge of different strategies strengthened, the general goals of creative drama work (empathy being the most frequently mentioned) were emphasized and feelings were brought into the classroom. Therefore, Laakso indicates that the results inspire confidence in drama, and highly recommends including, as a learning medium, in teacher education programs. In another study, Laakso (2004) found that drama was suitable for the learning of universals and concepts. Process drama proved also to have motivation-boosting effect.

Toivanen (2016, p. 227) highlights the efficiency of using drama in education as follows:

> …the use of drama in educational processes aids personal and social development, as well as the development of self-concept, self-discrepancy and a role-taking ability. Pupils who take drama classes enjoy school activities more, are much more willing to

participate in them, are better at problem solving and better at coping with stress. They have significantly more tolerance towards other people...The use of drama education can be seen as an alternative to scripted schooling and also an answer to the main challenges of the postmodern knowledge culture, which aims for deeper conceptual understanding by preparing students to create new knowledge.

The Use of Creative Drama to Develop Intercultural Competence in Foreign Language Classrooms

The reasons for frustration in language learning and failure in cross-cultural communication are increasingly seen to be cultural rather than linguistic in nature (Buttges, 1991; Salopelto, 2008). For successful intercultural competence, it is crucial to provide a much greater understanding of language, culture and language education (Buttges, 1991). While there is more interest in studies that integrate language and culture, there is still a growing need for intercultural competence, because in the globalizing world, cultures interact more either due to immigration or technological developments.

Students should learn to communicate in foreign language use contexts, and to understand and respect other cultures, as well as learn skills specific to the target language culture (Salopelto, 2008). Foreign language teaching has the potential to give the student a new perspective on their own language and culture.

Understanding a language involves the knowledge of grammar, phonology, lexis and cultural characteristics; in other words, to communicate internationally also involves communicating interculturally (MEB, 2016). The Turkish Ministry of Education thus indicates the need to develop intercultural competence as well as foreign language.

In foreign language teaching "the notion of culture adopted is prescriptive and static and it assumes that the learning of culture is something to tag on after grammatical structures and vocabulary have been covered" (Cunico, 2005, p. 22). This approach to culture reflects the belief that understanding a foreign culture is mainly a cognitive process. In this view, culture is a blend of factual and stable knowledge, with values and beliefs uniformly shared amongst speakers of the same language. In contrast, from the ethnographer's perspective, culture is dynamic and contextually defined in terms of the social practices within a particular language community, and it is this conceptualization which is more relevant to the foreign language student (Cunico, 2005: 23). Cunico's (2005) approach to drama stresses the notion of identity, and its close link to language use, viewing "culture" in terms of "practices" rather than knowledge.

Similarly, Salopelto (2008) draws attention to the lack of studies which utilize drama in developing intercultural competence in foreign language teaching. Drama can support the acquisition of empathy, which is an integral element of intercultural competence (Salopelto, 2008). In his action research, he developed some experimental materials. The qualitative and quantitative findings of this study demonstrated that drama increases emphatic skills and develops intercultural competence.

In the same vein, the lesson plan below exemplifies how intercultural competence can be developed through creative drama in foreign language classrooms.

A Sample Lesson Plan to Develop Intercultural Competence through Creative Drama in Foreign Language Classrooms

Group: Preparatory class (30 students)

Subject: Intercultural Topics (Different meanings of mimes and gestures to express in different cultures)

Time: 4 lesson hours

Method: Creative Drama

Techniques: Role on the wall, improvisation, hot seating, consciousness alley, flashback, split screen, writing in role.

Materials and Equipment: Equipment playing music (Golden Leaves by the Passengers), wall pictures showing cultural clues related to England, blank papers for writing letters.

Objectives:
- To practice different cultural mimes and gestures
- To learn cultural differences
- To learn some expressions related to going abroad, travelling
- To develop speaking and writing skills
- To increase intercultural competence
- To enhance creativity

The process
Warm-up Stage:
1. The teacher divides the class into two groups. One student from each group takes a card describing a mime or gesture in a specific culture, and without showing the card, performs the action. The rest of that student's group has to find the meaning of the gesture. After everyone has a turn, the winning group is announced.
2. The teacher asks the students to look at the pictures on the wall, and asks them to guess the country the y represent, which is England. Then the teacher asks the students to close their eyes and listen to a piece of slow music while also they listen to a poem on loneliness. After this the students to discuss what they have felt, and whether they have experienced loneliness in a different culture/country.
3. The teacher tells the students to portray a character who has just arrived in England for the first time. They form the character using role on the wall technique. First of all, they name their Turkish character. The teacher asks some questions about the character, and they brainstorm answer. After that, the most frequent answers are written on the board.

A Sample Lesson Plan to Develop Intercultural Competence through Creative Drama in Foreign Language Classrooms
Enactment
1. The teacher tells the class that the character they have created (for example, Ali, but in every class this name will be different) goes to England for the first time. His English is not good and he experiences a problem at the airport. The teacher forms groups of three, and asks the groups to improvise this situation.
2. The teacher tells the students to work in randomly selected new groups of six students. They will improvise a situation in which Ali is misunderstood, and had a problem related to cultural differences. The problem is related to different cultural meanings of gestures and facial expressions. This technique is similar to hot seating interrogation by all the others.
3. The students form groups of six and use the split screen technique. They will improvise a situation in which Ali will have dinner with his friends in London, and the other screen, in which his family in Turkey will have dinner. The two scenes will allow discussion of cultural differences.
4. The teacher asks the class to form an alley consisting of two lines of students facing each other. A volunteer student will play Ali, who is undecided whether to return to Turkey or stay in London. While Ali is passing through the consciousness alley, the other students give their opinions to help him to make a decision.
5. The teacher asks the class to form groups of five. They will start in the present and they return to the main character's past to understand why he had decided to go abroad (Flashback technique).
Evaluation Stage
1. The teacher asks the students to think of themselves as Ali, and write a letter to a friend in Turkey, focusing on cultural differences between Turkey and England. The letters are collected and distributed randomly on the floor. Everyone picks a letter and they are read aloud.
2. The teacher asks some questions related to the lesson and these are discussed in detail by the students sitting in the circle.

Conclusion

Although the importance of intercultural competence is agreed on, no clear path has been developed to achieve this. This chapter provided some practical ideas after discussing the theoretical framework related to intercultural competence and creative drama. Creative drama can facilitate the journey to intercultural competence. Creative drama is defined as an improvisational, non-exhibitionist process-centered form of drama in which students enact, imagine and reflect upon human experiences (Heathcote, 1991). It increases participants' emphatic skills, bringing insights into different characters and situations which they have never before experienced. The spontaneity of the improvisations increases the participants' creativity, and prepares them for real life situations. It also helps the students to develop verbal and non-verbal language as well as aesthetic skills. With these characteristics, creative drama can be an effective method of bringing cultural differences to life, and equipping the students with the crucial 21st century intercultural skills. In conclusion, creative drama represents an effective alternative approach to developing intercultural competence specifically in foreign language classrooms.

References

Adıgüzel, H. Ö., Üstündağ, T., & Öztürk, A. (2007). *İlköğretimde drama.* Eskişehir: Anadolu Üniversitesi Açık Öğretim Fakültesi Yayınları.

Adıgüzel, Ö. (2006). Yaratıcı drama kavramı, bileşenleri ve aşamaları. *Yaratıcı Drama Dergisi, 1*(1), 17–30.

Adıgüzel, Ö. (2010). *Eğitimde Yaratıcı Drama.* Ankara: Naturel Yayıncılık.

Ataman, M. (2009). *Türkçe derslerinde kullanılabilecek yaratıcı etkinlikler ve yaratıcı yazma örnekleri (Yaratıcı Drama Yöntemi ile).* Ankara: Kök Yayıncılık.

Huber, J., & Reynolds, C. (Eds.). (2014) *Developing intercultural competence through education.* Strasbourg: Council of Europe.

Bushman, J. H. (2001). *Teaching English creatively.* Springfield, IL: Charles C Thomas, Publisher LTD.

Buttges, D. (1991). Mediating languages and cultures: The social and intercultural dimension restored. In D. Buttjes & M. Byram (Eds.), *Mediating languages and cultures: Towards an intercultural theory of foreign language education multilingual matters (Series)*(3–17). Clevedon: Multilingual Matters.

Byram, M., Gribkova, B., & Starkey, H. (2002). *Developing the intercultural dimension in language teaching: A practical introduction for teachers.* Strasbourg: Council of Europe.

Cunico, S. (2005). Teaching language and intercultural competence through drama: Some suggestions for a neglected resource. *The Language Learning Journal, 31*(1), 21–29. doi: 10.1080/09571730585200051

DiNapoli, R. (2003). Towards natural engagement in nonexhibitional dramatic role-plays. *Iberica, 6,* 15–38.

Güryay, B. (2012). The use of creative drama. In F. Çubukçu (Ed.), *Teaching skills* (pp. 209–225). Ankara: Nobel.

Heathcote, D. (1991). *Collected writings on education and drama*. In L. Johnson & C. O'Neill (Eds.). Evanston, IL: Northwestern University Press.

Kavcar, C. (2006). Örgün eğitimde dramatizasyon. In H. Ö. Adıgüzel (Ed.), *Yaratıcı Drama 1985-1998 Yazılar* (pp. 18–28). Ankara: Naturel Yayınları.

Laakso, E. (1996). Reflections in a lake. What do prospective teachers experience during a period of educational drama. In J. Somers (Ed.), *Drama and theatre in education* (pp. 245–246). North York: Captus Press.

Laakso, E. (2004). *Draamakokemusten äärellä: prosessidraaman oppimispotentiaali opettajaksi opiskelevien kokemusten valossa* (No. 238). Jyväskylän yliopisto.

McCaslin, N. (1990). *Creative Drama in the Classroom*. Studio City, CA: Players Plays.

MEB (2016). T.C. Milli Eğitim Bakanlığı Hazırlık Sınıfı Bulunan Ortaöğretim Kurumları İngilizce Dersi Öğretim Programı http://mufredat.meb.gov.tr/ ProgramDetay.aspx?PID=783 (last retrieved on 13.12.2019).

National core curriculum for basic education (NCC, 2016). https://www.oph. fi/sites/default/files/documents/new-national-core-curriculum-for-basic-education.pdf (last retrieved on 13.12.2019).

Neelands, J., & Goode, T. (2010). *Structuring drama work: A Handbook of available forms in theatre and drama*. Cambridge, United Kingdom: Cambridge University Press.

Salopelto, H. (2008). *Intercultural competence through drama. A teaching experiment*. Unpublished master's thesis, University of Jyväskylä, Finland.

San, İ. (2006). Yaratıcı dramanın eğitsel boyutları. In H. Ö.Adıgüzel (Ed.), *Yaratıcı Drama 1985-1998 Yazılar* (pp. 113–122). Ankara: Naturel Yayınları.

San, İ. (2008). Adlandırmayı Değiştirmeyelim. *Çağdaş Drama Derneği, Yaratıcı Drama Dergisi*, 1–5, 103–115.

Toivanen, T. (2016). Drama education in the finnish school system–Past, present and future. In H. Niemi, A. Toom, & A. Kallioniemi (Eds.), *Miracle of education* (pp. 227–240). Rotterdam: Sense Publishers.

Winston, J. (2004). *Drama and English at the heart of the curriculum, primary and middle years*. London: David Fulton Publishers.

Yılmaz, N. (2010). Etkinliklerin Çatısı. In A. Kırkar & N. Yılmaz (Eds.), *İlköğretim derslerinde yaratıcı drama uygulamaları* (pp. 15–19). Istanbul: Çınar Yayınl

Gonca Yangın Ekşi and Asuman Aşık

6 Raising Intercultural Awareness through Technology

In a challenging era of globalization, language learners are required to master various competencies and skills to keep abreast with the demands of the 21st century. Intercultural competence is one of the key competences that language learners need to improve. Moreover, with the advancements in technology, language teaching has undergone a significant shift on the use of digital materials, Web 2.0 and medium of instruction. It is acknowledged that technology has several affordances on raising cultural awareness and increasing intercultural communicative competence of foreign language learners. Therefore, this chapter aims to explore how technology can be used to increase intercultural awareness of foreign language learners. The advent of the internet and Web 2.0 in ICT field has been significant in the use of technology for intercultural competence. In this regard, this book chapter will present a concise historical background of technology use for cultural awareness such as social media use, online games, podcasting etc. With this background in mind, the chapter will mainly focus on the current implementations of technology use which contribute considerably to increase intercultural awareness.

The recent trends include the use of computer-mediate communication and telecollaboration in particular for language teaching purposes. The use of computer-mediated communication (CMC) tools of today with a wide range of text-based, oral and multimodal mediums like social networking environments, mobile devices and video conferencing has changed the understanding of social participation and collaboration (Guerin, Cigognini, & Pettenati, 2010). With the examples from CMC studies and theoretical background in the chapter, the telecollaborative practices will be discussed to provide guidelines for language teachers on how to use technology for raising intercultural awareness. Telecollaboration is defined as "the use of online communication tools to bring together language learners in different countries for the development of collaborative project work and intercultural exchange" (O'Dowd & Ritter, 2006, p. 1). Recently, there is a growing interest in conducting telecollaborative projects by universities throughout the world. This chapter will also present the latest projects on telecollaboration and how they contribute to the intercultural competence. Some sample tasks and best practices from the current projects will also be presented. Moreover, the chapter also aims to offer practical suggestions and pedagogical implications for language teachers so that they can find their own way to use technology for raising cultural awareness of their students.

Introduction

The 21st century is characterized with increased opportunities in contact and travel in a globalized world and the everyday lives of people being interwoven with the use of technology. The ever-spreading use of digital technologies is transforming every aspect of our lives, from communication to relationships, from education to workplace and so on. Digital technologies also changed the construct of space and distance. Ease of access to information and communication via digital technologies has made space and place *increasingly augmented, hybridized, layered,* or *mediated* (Duggan, 2018). Technology changed the way we communicate and basically communication technologies include the Internet, social media, multimedia, e-mail, telephone and other sound-based and video-based communication means such as Skype, video conferencing, Google Docs, blogs, wikis or other computer mediated communication (CMC) tools.

As increasingly more people are contacting each other in every corner of the world, Intercultural Communicative Competence (ICC) has become more important. More and more people share ideas, consume and create content and interact with each other, English being the international contact language. Therefore, learning English should also involve some cross-cultural awareness raising. The ability to communicate across linguistic and cultural borders successfully and efficiently does not solely depend on a certain level of proficiency in English, but rather on intercultural awareness. That is, developing an ability to understand cultures, including one's own and others', especially differences and attitudes and values. People interact across borders and cultures and "successful intercultural communication is a matter of highest importance if humankind and society are to survive" (Samovar, Porter, & McDaniel, 2006). This chapter focuses on increasing cultural awareness using technology in English language teaching with reference to globalization and intercultural communication. The possibilities, challenges and limitations of using information and communication technologies (or ICTs) in the development of cross-cultural awareness needs to be investigated.

Language Learning and Culture

What is taught as culture in the language classroom has changed throughout the years. Traditionally it was the high culture with a capital C, that is, works of art and literature. Short literary works and poems were introduced, and the aim was the ability to read, understand and interpret such literary work. Later there was a shift from capital C to small c. With the communicative approach in the 1970s, it was the small c culture that was emphasized in the language classroom such as the social aspects of everyday life, holidays and customs. Rather than describing or giving factual information about aspects of culture, authentic texts and realia were introduced to the learners. Later, with the impact of globalization, the need to train learners to use English as a lingua franca and develop their intercultural awareness has emerged. Language learners need strategies for interpreting cultures and languages when they communicate.

When learning a foreign language, familiarity with the culture of those who speak the language as a mother tongue is usually taken for granted. To achieve successful communication across cultures, it is necessary to understand culture specific norms of interaction, values and thoughts (Saville-Troike, 2003) because it is sometimes possible that linguistically correct sentences can cause misunderstanding, or even offence in a different culture (Schulz, 2007).

Alptekin points that, "learning a foreign language becomes a kind of enculturation, where one acquires new cultural frames of reference and a new world view, reflecting those of the target language culture and its speakers" (2002, p. 58). Learning a foreign language involves learning aspects of culture. As to English however, one should take into account its role as Lingua Franca. As an international contact language, English has spread all over the world. The number of nonnative speakers has exceeded that of native speakers. That is, learning English does not only enable learners to speak to native speakers but also to those who speak English as a second or foreign language. As a result of the global spread of English worldwide, American or British cultures may no longer be the solely relevant cultures in language teaching and learning (Alptekin, 2002). Kachru's Circles English (1992) illustrates the current sociolinguistic profile of English language on a world scale. An ever-increasing number of speakers of English can be classified as those from Inner Circle Countries, Outer Circle Countries, and Expanding Circle Countries, respectively first language (L1), second language (L2) and foreign language (FL) speakers. Even the target culture, the Inner Circle, is broader than British or American cultures. These speakers come from very different backgrounds. Therefore, a broader view of cultural understanding is necessary for speakers from every corner of the world to interact with one another rather than focusing on a limited target culture.

The multi-faceted role of English on the international stage assumes pedagogical challenges in English language teaching. For millions of learners English is no longer learned to understand American or British cultural values to function within the target societies. The motivation for learning a second or foreign language learning has also changed. The simple integrative/instrumental dichotomy in language learning motivation needs to be expanded. Integrative motivation, which is defined as an individual's interest in and positive attitudes towards the target language group would be too limited because many English interactions around the world occur across the three concentric circles defined by Kachru. In several interactions, non-native speakers use English as the international contact language and there is little or no identifiable target community. In such cases, English means a language that connects the learners to "foreigners" around the world, with whom they can communicate in English (Yasima, 2002). Hence, a broader sense of cultural awareness appears to be vital in uses of English across the world.

Technology and Cultural Awareness in Language Teaching

It is often acknowledged that language and culture are indeed inseparable (Brown, 2000). Elements of the target culture such as aspects of everyday life, behavioral norms, traditions and values as well as literary works and artifacts should be incorporated even from the earlier levels of language learning. ICT tools can be used to incorporate linguistically and culturally authentic texts in language instruction. Genuine contact into the target culture is also possible through online exchanges. Computer Mediated Communication (CMC) offers many opportunities for peer-to-peer interaction, which in turn helps improve language proficiency as well as cultural awareness.

The world is ever-connected in every corner through the Internet and Web 2.0 tools. More people from different linguistic and cultural backgrounds than ever before are interacting with one another. Hence, both language learning and cultural understanding can be facilitated through technology.

The Internet provides contact with the native speakers or other speakers and access to authentic materials and media. Such online authentic resources might contribute to reading ability and the listening skill. They are also an invaluable source for learning about the target culture and other cultures. Social media platforms such as Facebook, blogs, chat and online forums provide contextualized real language experience through negotiation. Multiplayer online games also present rich international and intercultural contact. Engaging with speakers of other languages in online exchanges might be authentic communication and conflict and miscommunication that can occur can provide powerful learning opportunities. However, merely providing students with technology is not enough to increase cultural awareness. The question is what teachers should do to cultivate cultural awareness.

Computer Mediated Communication (CMC) and Intercultural Awareness

Computer-mediated communication (CMC) is defined as "communication that takes place between human beings via the instrumentality of computers" (Herring, 1996, p. 1). CMC tools (e.g., e-mail, Instant Messaging [IM], teleconferencing, Skype, video conferencing etc.) allow people to converse across space and time. CMC has two modalities: synchronous computer-mediated communication (SCMC) and asynchronous computer-mediated communication (ACMC). The former refers to the relatively immediate occurrence of communication (Abrams, 2003; Terhune, 2016; Zeng, 2017) whereas the latter refers that there is a time interval between the responses sent by the interlocutors in a communication. Below is a non-exhaustive list of CMC tools: e-mail, Facebook, Twitter, Skype, Second Life, Google Handouts, blogging, wikis, online multiplayer games, chat, online forums, Moodle, and other social networking sites.

A considerable amount of research on CMC focuses on interaction in CMC environments and language learners' identity construction in CMC interactions. Intercultural communication is another line of research in CMC studies. Le and Markey (2014) investigated the effects of the use of digital technology on the learners' views about intercultural learning and peer feedback. Jin (2015) also adopted Facebook in her action research for facilitating intercultural interactions between Korean EFL learners and American undergraduate students. Özdemir (2017) conducted a research study on how Facebook affects intercultural communicative effectiveness among EFL learners. Chen and Yang (2016) investigated the effectiveness of a project (UBOD) on the development of Taiwanese EFL learners' ICC and language skills.

Today, people all around the world participate in chatrooms, video conferencing and forum and discussion lists and join global games, log in to virtual worlds, read or author international reading blogs, and connect partners or build international teams in the business world taking advantage of CMC tools. However, bridging time and space and bringing people from different nations together does not guarantee that their cultures are similarly bridged (Olson &

Olson, 2000). Communication breakdowns are likely to occur due to differences in cultural and social norms, conversational conventions, work styles, and so on.

CMC provides construction of meaning and learning through "active engagement, discovery learning, sociocultural context, and co-construction of knowledge in knowledge communities or communities of practice" (Luppicini, 2002, p. 89). With a sociocognitive angle, CMC may have a more positive effect on the acquisition of cultural awareness of students (Zeiss & Isabelli-Garcia, 2005) and engages students in learning through social interaction and thus allows for awareness about a culture other than their own (Liu, 2002).

Using CMC to interact with native speakers in foreign language creates real audience, communication and authentic language experience. CMC can also shed light on existing stereotypes and promote detailed views of the host culture (Furstenberg, Levet, English, & Maillet, 2001; Itakura, 2004). Internet-based communication can also serve to remove stereotypes through providing genuine communication between the members of different cultures and insights via CMC. Asynchronous CMC, e-mail or other forms, provide an authentic language experience and a more personalized learning (Silva, Meagher, Valenzuela, & Crenshaw, 1996) for students and allows them to develop empathy with their peers in other cultures. With the genuine communication opportunities CMC provides, language is the means and not just the end of the learning process.

Telecollaboration and ICC

CMC has been conducive to building communities for collaboration and creating opportunities for language learning. One of the common uses of CMC in education is through telecollaborative exchanges. Recent studies have shown that telecollaboration offers several considerable benefits for improved language skills, ICC, digital literacy and 21st century skills (Guth & Helm, 2010, Lee & Markey, 2014; Schenker, 2012). It has been acknowledged that telecollaboration should be included in foreign language teaching to improve ICC (Çiftçi & Savaş, 2018; O'Dowd, 2016, Thorne, 2010). Since intercultural (communicative) competence (ICC) is the ability of language learners to communicate and negotiate successfully with people from different backgrounds (Byram, 1997), telecollaboration might serve as an effective medium to improve ICC of language learners. telecollaboration, one of the virtual exchange initiatives, is defined by O'Dowd (2018) as "the engagement of groups of learners in extended periods of online intercultural interaction and collaboration with partners from other cultural contexts or geographical locations as an integrated part of their educational programs and under the guidance of educators and/or expert facilitators" (p. 1).

Earlier models of telecollaboration were designed around the native speaker as the ideal interlocutor who gives cultural information and feedback on linguistic competence to language learners during online collaborative exchanges. However, in the era of EFL, it has been asserted that nonnative speakers communicate mostly with other nonnative speakers in multiple various contexts, which cannot be limited only between a native and a nonnative speaker. In this regard, new telecollaboration approaches have emerged. Helm and Guth (2016) ascertain that exchanges in today's world, with a much more flexible quality, may be multilateral and multilingual for multiple purposes.

Telecollaboration has gained its popularity in the last decade as it offers considerable opportunities to language learners to communicate with people from diverse contexts and backgrounds, which may not be possible for many language learners. Telecollaboration eliminates the barriers between language learners through online exchanges, which also foster "internationalization at home" strategies by eliminating the barriers of geographical distances.

For the improvement of ICC skills and language skills of language learners, telecollaborative projects have created innovative ways by designing and implementing online intercultural collaborative environments (Çiftçi & Savaş, 2018). Furthermore, Sadler and Dooly (2016) describe telecollaborative learning as "an embedded, dialogic process that supports geographically distanced collaborative work through social interaction, involving a/synchronous communication technology so that participants co-produce mutual objective(s) and share knowledge-building" (p. 402).

With respect to the growing interest in the field, several projects on telecollaboration and virtual exchange were funded by the European Commission. Thus, in order to exemplify accessible and practical uses of telecollaborative exchanges, some of the recent projects on telecollaboration are summarized below:

1. *The Integrating Telecollaborative Networks in Higher Education (INTENT) Project*: It aims to increase awareness of telecollaboration around the academic world and to look for ways for its integration into university education. The UNICollaboration platform explained below was one of the outcomes of this project.
2. *EVALuating and Upscaling telecollaborative Teacher Education (EVALUATE)*: It aims to focus on the impact of virtual exchange on students in initial teacher education across Europe.
3. *Erasmus+ Virtual Exchange (EVE)*: the European Commission focuses on the potential of virtual exchange by launching a flagship program which

aims to expand the reach and scope of the Erasmus+ program via virtual exchange. The program provides learners a variety of virtual exchange initiatives.

4. *Unicollaboration* (www.unicollaboration.org) is a cross-disciplinary professional organization for telecollaboration and virtual exchange in Higher Education. It aims to promote the development and integration of research and practice in telecollaboration and virtual exchange across all disciplines and subject areas in higher education. Individual and institutional memberships are available.

With the emergence of several telecollaborative projects, several suggestions for instruction were made to improve ICC through telecollaboration and to assess its outcomes. For example, O'Dowd and Waire (2009) with a review of 40 studies on telecollaborative tasks suggested a design process for foreign language telecollaborative projects and tasks. They suggested three categories: (a) information exchange tasks which include sharing information about biographies, interests and cultures among partners, (b) comparison and analysis in which students critically compare some cultural products such as newspapers and books, (c) collaborative tasks through which students are asked to develop a joint product through collaboration.

Based on O'Dowd and Ware's (2009) framework, Ferreira-Lopes, Bezanilla and Elexpuru (2018) developed a theory-informed task sequence to facilitate the integration of telecollaboration into university courses for the development of Intercultural Competence. The task sequence is adaptable and flexible for diverse contexts and it includes the following characteristics:

1. First, non-specific activities such as ice-breakers, comparison and analysis and group contracts need to be conducted to build trust among group members, then any kind of subject-related activities should be given.
2. The technology tools such as Google classroom, Moodle, Google Survey and Google forms can be used since they are open access and have user-friendly characteristics.
3. Several instruments for both quantitative and qualitative assessment such as self-evaluation, videos, reflection tasks and group reports can be used to evaluate intercultural competence.
4. The telecollaborative task sequence is suggested to be gradually integrated into the core subject of the course rather than as a supplementary material.

For an effective implementation of a telecollaborative exchange to improve ICC of language learners, suggestions from previous studies were gathered and provided below (Ferreira-Lopes, Bezanilla, & Elexpuru, 2018; Helm & Guth, 2016; O'Dowd & Ware, 2009).

1. Task-based language learning is mostly suitable as a methodology of language teaching in telecollaborative exchanges. Task cycle should be planned in detail. For example, stages such as preparatory pre-task, interactive task and reflective post-task can be designed.
2. Before the exchange, teachers should specify a structured outline with specific objectives, tasks and a calendar in collaboration.
3. Teachers and students should prepare some guidelines about the implementation which include day and time, the type of CMC tool (synchronous or and asynchronous), expectations from each partner and how much workload is needed.
4. There should be compatibility in the implementation of the task between teachers, courses and institutional procedures. For example, teachers should discuss whether the task will be supplementary or integrated to the coursework, will be graded or not, will include any flexibility, will require equal workload from the partners, will include which tools. Teachers and students negotiate upon these principles since all of these issues may cause imbalanced participation and commitment.

Furthermore, based on the experiences in telecollaboration, Müller-Hartman, O'Dowd et al. (2018) list the platforms and communication tools for telecollaborative exchanges as can be seen in Tab. 1.

Sample Telecollaborative Tasks

There are several tasks and projects that are accessible through Unicollaboration platform. The following tasks were taken from the task databank on www.unicollaboration.org/index.php/tasks-databank/. The task databank is organized with a title, description and CEFR level. The following tasks are given to exemplify how telecollaboration may improve intercultural competence.

Example 1:

Task title: Chain stories (reported by University Warwick)

Description: Groups of students in two different institutions collaborate together to produce a short story which continues from an opening line given to them by the tutor. Using Google docs, the students contribute to a story in their own language as well as one in the target language. They can all edit and add comments, correcting language and changing the direction of the storyline.

Tab. 1: Some Resources and Tools for Telecollaborative Exchanges

Platforms to find telecollaborative partners and resources	Communication tools for Telecollaborative Exchanges
1. UNICollaboration: www. unicollaboration.eu 2. Telecollaboration for Intercultural Language Acquisition (TILA): http:// www.tilaproject.eu/moodle/ 3. Cultura: https://cultura.mit.edu/	• Blogger: https://www.blogger.com/home • Google Drive: drive.google.com • Edmodo: edmodo.com
4. EPals: http://www.epals.com/ 5. Etwinning: http://www.etwinning.net/ 6. Schools Online: http://schoolsonline. britishcouncil.org/ 7. IEARN: https://iearn.org/	• Schoology: www.schoology.com/ • Skype: skype.com • Vyew: vyew.com • Wikispaces: wikispaces.com • Google Hangouts: www.google.com/ hangouts • Canvas: www.canvasvle.co.uk • Moodle: www.moodle.org

Target competencies: language competence, intercultural skills, online communication skills, teaching skills, media literacy

Level: Any

Example 2:

Task title: Cultural Speaking Exchange (by Universidad Europea Miguel de Cervantes)

Description: You have to have at least four sessions of approx. 40 minutes where you will speak 20 minutes in Spanish and 20 minutes in English. You have to write a paper in English with what you have talked about during these sessions. What have you learned? What has surprised you most?

1st session: Present yourself, what are you studying, why are you studying this, do you have any siblings, where do they live, etc. The university: What is it like. Describe your university, how is normal university day, your subjects, your favorite subjects, why?

2nd session: Free time. Talk about hobbies, what do you like to do in your free time, what type of music do you like, movies, museums, cooking, etc. Do you travel? Where have you been, where would you like to go, why or why not, what do you like to do when you travel, etc.

3rd session: Life in your hometown. Talk about your culture, traditions or food of your country. What do you think your partner would enjoy from your country? What would s/he not, if s/he came to your city, where would you take him/her? Why? Where would you not take him/her? Why not?

4th session. Stereotypes and recap. Talk about things about your country you think would seem strange or that would interest your partner if s/he came to Spain/Valladolid or USA. Talk about what the average Spaniard/American would know about the other country.

Final project:

You have to write a small essay about your cultural exchange experience. Briefly write about your partner and what you have learned from this experience. What was the most interesting part? What was the most surprising part? How did you feel about communicating? Was is it difficult? Did it get better? How did you solve the communications problems if you had any? Did you learn anything about your own culture or identity?

Level: B1, B2

Example 3

Task Title: SWAP Meeting (by University of Pamplona)

Description: In a globalized world with the great amount of useful ICT that the internet provides, all aspects of daily life, as well as all the disciplines that have changed drastically. Here can be included the educational field. The classes continue changing from a teacher-centered approach to a more student-centered in which they are the focus of the classes with their active participation and responsibility about their own learning process. That is the reason why, this project aims at developing different skills such as: language skills, communication skills, critical thinking, intercultural competence, among others of the foreign languages community of the university of Pamplona by means of the development of three sessions called "swap meetings" in which students from around the world participate in a unicollaboration class by exchanging knowledge and cultural aspects of their hometowns.

Language of task instructions: English

Target Group: Any

Level: B1, B2

Type: Information exchange

Estimated Duration: Four sessions

Topic: Culture, languages, facts, habits, food, stereotypes, environment and consumerism

Objectives:

Main objective: To encourage students' intercultural competence by the exchange of cultural facts about their countries

Specific Objectives:

– To carry out collaborative sessions in order to practice ESL competences through the use of the unicollaboration web page and the use of video calls.
– To help participants become aware of the importance of eco-friendly habits over consumerism.
– To discuss about different cultural traits around the world

Conclusion

With the increasing demand on 21st century skills in education, technology provides several opportunities for foreign language learning contexts. In a world of ELF, language learners need more authentic experiences with other non-native or native speakers of English, which is possible in many ways through technology. In this regard, this chapter aims at exploring how to raise cultural awareness of language learners by using technology in English language teaching in terms of globalization and intercultural communication.

In order to increase ICC of language learners, the CMC tools with a wide range of tools (blogs, Google hangouts, social networking sites, online games etc.) are accessible and promising for many creative and productive uses. In particular, today, telecollaboration through CMC tools is of increasing interest to several language teachers, learners and institutions. With the aforementioned uses of CMC and telecollaboration, language teachers can organize tasks with other teachers from other countries. These tasks may contain introducing their own culture, sharing information and creating a new product in collaboration with their partners from other countries. Through these telecollaborative exchanges, both teachers and learners can increase their ICC and be more open-minded for other cultures and languages.

References

Alptekin, C. (2002). Towards intercultural communicative competence in ELT. *ELT Journal, 56*(1), 57–64.

Brown, H. D. (2000). *Principles of language learning and teaching.* New York: Longman.

Byram, M. (1997). *Teaching and assessing intercultural communicative competence.* Clevedon, UK: Multilingual Matters.

Çiftçi, E. Y., & Savaş, P. (2017). The role of telecollaboration in language and intercultural learning: A synthesis of studies published between 2010 and 2015. *ReCALL, 30*(3), 278–298. doi:10.1017/S0958344017000313

Duggan, M. (2018). The everyday reality of a digitalizing world. In T. Felgenhauer & K. Gäbler (Eds.), *Geographies of Digital Culture.* New York: Routledge.

Ferreira-Lopes, L., Bezanilla, M. J., & Elexpuru, I. (2018). Integrating intercultural competence development into the curriculum through telecollaboration. A task sequence proposal for higher education. *RED. Revista de Educacion a Distancia, 58,* 1–36.

Furstenberg, G., Levet, S., English, K., & Maillet, K. (2001). Giving a virtual voice to the silent language of culture: The Cultura project. *Language Learning & Technology, 15*(1), 55–102.

Guerin, E. M. C., Cigognini, M. E., & Pettenati, M. C. (2010). Learner 2.0. In S. Gut & F. Helm (Eds.), *Telecollaboration 2.0 language literacies and intercultural learning in the 21st century* (pp. 199–218). Bern: Peter Lang.

Guth, S., & Helm, F. (Eds.) (2010). *Telecollaboration 2.0: Language and intercultural learning in the 21st Century* (pp. 13–35). Bern, Switzerland: Peter Lang.

Helm, F., & Guth, S. (2016). Telecollaboration and language learning. In F. Farr & L. Murray (Eds.), *The Routledge handbook of language learning and technology* (pp. 241–254). London: Routledge.

Kachru, B. (1992). Teaching World Englishes. In B. Kachru (Ed.), *The other tongue: English across cultures* (2nd ed., pp. 355–364). Urbana: University of Illinois Press.

Lee, L., & Markey, A. (2014). A study of learners' perceptions of online intercultural exchange through Web 2.0 technologies. *ReCALL, 26*(3), 281–297. doi: 10.1017/S0958344014000111

Liu, P. (2002). Developing an e-pal partnership: A school-based international activity. *Childhood Education, 79*(2), 81–88.

Luppicini, R. J. (2002). Toward a conversation system modeling research methodology for studying computer-mediated learning communities. *Journal of Distance Education, 17/2,* 87–101.

Müller-Hartman, A., O'Dowd, R., & colleagues from the EVALUATE Group. (2017). *A training manual on telecollaboration for teacher trainers.* https://www.evaluateproject.eu/evlt-data/uploads/2017/09/Training-Manual_EVALUATE.pdf.

O'Dowd, R. (2016). Emerging trends and new directions in telecollaborative learning. *CALICO Journal, 33*(3), 291–310. doi: 10.1558/cj.v33i3.30747

O'Dowd, R. (2018). From telecollaboration to virtual exchange: State-of-the-art and the role of UNICollaboration in moving forward. *Journal of Virtual Exchange, 1,* 1–23. Research-publishing.net. doi: 10.14705/rpnet.2018.jve.1

O'Dowd, R., & Ritter, M. (2006). Understanding and working with "failed communication" in telecollaborative exchanges. *CALICO Journal*, *23*(3), 623–642.

O'Dowd, R., & Waire, P. (2009). Critical issues in telecollaborative task design. *Computer Assisted Language Learning*, *22*(2), 173–188. doi: 10.1080/09588220902778369

Sadler, R., & Dooly, M. (2016). Twelve years of telecollaboration: What we have learnt. *ELT Journal*, *70*(4), 401–413. doi: 10.1093/elt/ccw041

Samovar, L. A., Porter, R. E., & McDaniel, E. R. (2006). *Intercultural communication: A reader* (11th ed.). Belmont: Thomson/Wadsworth.

Saville-Troike, M. (2003). *The ethnography of communication*. Oxford: Blackwell Publishing.

Schenker, T. (2012). Intercultural competence and cultural learning through telecollaboration. *CALICO Journal*, *29*(3), 449–470. doi: 10.11139/cj.29.3.449-470

Schulz, R. A. (2007). The challenge of assessing cultural understanding in the context of foreign language instruction. *Foreign Language Annals*, *40*(1), 9–26.

Silva, P., Meager, M. E., Valenzuale, M., & Crenshaw, S. W. (1996). Email: Real life classroom experiences with foreign languages. *Learning and Leading with Technology*, *23*, 10–12.

Thorne, S. (2010). The "intercultural turn" and language learning in the crucible of new media. In S. Guth & F. Helm (Eds.), *Telecollaboration 2.0: Language, literacies and intercultural learning in the 21st century* (pp. 139–164). New York: Peter Lang.

Yashima, T. (2002). Willingness to communicate in a second language: The Japanese EFL context. *Modern Language Journal*, *86*, 54–66.

Zeiss, E., & Isabelli-García, C. L. (2005). The role of asynchronous computer mediated communication on enhancing cultural awareness. *Computer Assisted Language Learning*, *18*(3), 151–169. doi: 10.1080/09588220500173310

Claudia Nickolson and Arda Arikan

7 Developing Intercultural Competence through Movies

Developing Global Literacy: Intercultural Competence through the Use of Films

In its simplest sense, the goal of intercultural competence, or global literacy, is to help students understand how to communicate with people who are different from them. Living in a global environment means that individuals from diverse cultures will need to know how to interact with each other, both face-to-face and online. Intercultural communication incorporates the study of communication patterns and cultural norms of diverse groups and students in English language classrooms can learn these norms in order to understand, appreciate and appropriately communicate with diverse others. In Byram's (1997) words, the task of understanding others' cultures is not an easy one although with the help of international media and popular culture among which films is the leading one, one can decipher the meanings of certain issues or behaviors portrayed with the help of what he calls a "skill of discovery" which:

> is the ability to recognise significant phenomena in a foreign environment and to elicit their meanings and connotations, and their relationship to other phenomena. Although the skill is essentially identical in different environments, it may be more difficult to operate in those which have least in common with the individual's country of origin, the so-called 'exotic' languages and cultures. However, given the power of international media and popular culture, it is likely that the individual will be able to identify some phenomena in the most distant environments, although it cannot be assumed that they have the same meaning and significance (p. 38).

One way to facilitate global literacy that can help us understand others' culture-specific behaviors and output is through the use of cross-cultural films in English language classrooms. According to Roell (2010), incorporating films in the curriculum invites students to both practice English and to develop intercultural competence through activities that "reveal how different dialects, forms of address, customs, taboos, and other cultural elements influence interaction among different groups" (p. 2).

Although there may be numerous benefits of developing intercultural competence in language education, three primary objectives for developing it are:

1. Leading students through an examination of their own perceptions, cultural subjectivities, and interactions with others,
2. Helping students develop empathy in understanding "the other" in their own socio-cultural context,
3. Helping students learn appropriate interpersonal communication skills for interacting with diverse others.

A rich and useful way to bring both literacy and cultural practices into the English language classroom is through the use of films. Nur (2014) highlights the value in using films as a tool for increasing students' cultural awareness, suggesting that they can help students to internalize situations which they might not have experienced personally. Activities and assignments can provide opportunities to develop group communication skills, practice writing skills and engage in critical thinking about intercultural norms in various contexts. Learning goals in these classrooms can focus on helping students gain insights into their own communication style and examine their perceptions of those whose communication style/culture may be different. Participants in activities can be encouraged to take the perspective of the "other" in order to achieve greater understanding and effectiveness. Stringer and Cassidy (2009) emphasize the importance of preparing students for learning engagements focused on cross-cultural communication/intercultural competence.

Prior to viewing films in the English language classroom, students should first discuss both generalizations and stereotypes. A generalization can be understood as a cultural norm; a pattern of communication used by the majority of people in a cultural group but not necessarily to everyone. When the cultural norm is applied to everyone in a group it has evolved into a stereotype. Hence, students' prior knowledge must include the negative effects of making generalizations and stereotyping on their psychological and mental well-being. Asking students to think and reflect on such questions like "How would you feel if. . .?" and "Has anyone ever . . .?" Similarly, students can be asked to complete such statements like "Turks love. . ." or "In Turkey, we. . ." and then interrogate the truth value of such statements by finding counter realities. For instance, while one student may suggest that "Turks love coffee", she will soon realize in her discussion with friends that not all Turks are fond of coffee. Hence, teachers should also caution students about stereotypes that we experience in real life and how they appear in films.

Cross-cultural miscommunication should also be examined in the classroom. Barriers may be related to preconceived notions and stereotypes that can occur when oversimplified characteristics are applied to a group of people or when we interpret a message by using our own cultural lens in a judgmental manner. Films are especially beneficial for cross-cultural learning because they offer an opportunity to connect to students emotionally as well as intellectually according to Summerfield (1993). When we experience intercultural contact through our senses and emotionally in a film, we can begin to understand it. Hence, not only what films show in terms of action, other aspects of it must be included in the final analysis such as music, dialogue, sound, and silence that are all "important to many of these works and to the feeling of embodied experience they produce" (Marks, 2000: xvi).

We have chosen three films with intercultural themes that can be utilized strategically to emphasize specific learning objectives related to intercultural topics. Learning experiences for students in secondary or college classrooms should reflect a balance of both theoretical and experiential learning or "doing" which can consist of participating in writing activities, role-plays, and critical analysis as active discussion in small groups.

Film #1: *Double Happiness* (1995)

Directed by Mina Shum, *Double Happiness* (1995) is a film that can be used to examine identity, parent-child conflict and having multiple and at times clashing points of view. The main character of the film is Jade Li, a young Chinese born Canadian actress who is experiencing pressure from her parents to marry within her culture. Pre-viewing activities may include learning more about marriage in its widest sense such as:

1. How do people in your family or country choose their future wives/husbands?
2. Are there rules about couples' meeting and spending time together before the marriage in your culture?
3. When or why are soon to be married couple criticized?

Post-viewing activities can support students' comprehension and provide opportunities to use English as they reflect on cultural norms that are portrayed in the film. Students can discuss some of the distinctions between the more traditional older generation, and the challenges this imposes on the younger generation as well as examine ways that Jade is forced to navigate her competing identities. Rather than judging the film characters' actions as "good" or "bad" students can engage in a role play where they can put themselves into a character's shoes and express their point of view. This could also be used as a writing exercise as an extension of the class discussion. Questions asked during this period can include:

1. How does Jade feel when she is pressured to marry someone she does not want to?
2. Do you feel pressured, for any reason, because of your family's involvement in your choices?
3. Is marriage a personal matter or a communal one? Support your claim through real life experiences and examples.
4. What would be your advice to Jade if you were her close friend? How should she behave among her family members to make them understand her view point.

Film #2: *Outsourced* (2007)

Directed by John Jeffcoat (2007), *Outsourced* (2007) is another film that can be described as a culture-clash romance. The main character, Todd, is fired from his call-center job in the U.S. and sent to India as a consultant to train his own replacement. The key to Todd's success in his new environment is adaptability; he must adapt to his hosts' culture, language, customs and behaviors. This film can provide a meaningful intercultural experience for student viewers especially when culture-shock and adaptability are concerned. Todd's experiences with Indian culture, food, language and marriage practices can be used as a basis for examining such cross-cultural adjustment. Teachers can use the following questions to facilitate discussion:

1. What are some cultural situations in the film that cause Todd discomfort? Have you ever had similar experiences with being a stranger in a strange new place?
2. How does Todd react to the kinds of personal questions that Aunt Ji asks? How does this compare to expectations in other cultures?
3. How can a lack of cultural competency lead to making mistakes while adjusting to a new culture?

Events portrayed in the film that highlight the contrast between individualist and collectivist cultures can also be examined with students from a critical perspective. Post viewing, students can critically examine whether the film promotes or helps to break down stereotypes. Furthermore, discussion on the difference between generalizations and stereotypes may take place in a scene-by-scene format. The following questions can help facilitate this discussion:

1. In the film, Todd is portrayed as culturally ignorant. How have stereotypes influenced Todd's perceptions of his Indian hosts? Examine stereotypes that you may have about other cultures.
2. Are there places (scenes) in the film where stereotypes are reinforced? Engage in a critical conversation about ways that films can reinforce stereotypes.
3. How might cultural misunderstandings provide opportunities to examine and break down misperceptions and stereotypes? Use examples from your own experience and discuss.

Film #3: *My Big Fat Greek Wedding* (2002)

Directed by Joel Zwick (2002), *My Big Fat Greek Wedding* (2002) is a romantic comedy that tells the story of a Greek-American family, and centers on Toula who, at the age of 30, is still unmarried. She works at the Greek restaurant owned by her parents and falls in love with Ian who is not Greek, after taking a job at her aunt's travel agency. Throughout the movie we see how Toula struggles to gain her family's acceptance of Ian as we experience her struggle to come to terms with her heritage and cultural identity. This film offers an opportunity for students to critically examine the notion of ethnocentrism, the belief that your own cultural group is superior to all others. Strong traditional cultural beliefs are conveyed through showing male and female actors in traditional gender roles all the while pressures to marry within one's own culture runs throughout the film. Critical viewing and discussion around this film can begin with these key questions and focal points:

1. Do you think that Toula's father displays ethnocentrism or ethnic pride throughout the movie? Are there ways that he is imposing his beliefs on others?
2. Discuss some of the ways that traditional cultural beliefs are creating an identity struggle for Toula. Have you experienced similar pressures related to gender roles or expectations from older generations?
3. What tensions does Toula experience in learning how to be an "American?"

Students can also examine the role of stereotypes; highlighted in the film when Ian's parents make a presumption that all non-European heritages are similar because they look like one another. Post-viewing discussion can also center on the role of compromise as a genuine concept in intercultural communication. For example, Ian consents to be baptized as Greek, thereby giving up a part of himself in order to gain acceptance from Toula's family. Thus, consider the following topics with students:

1. Revisit the role of stereotypes or presumptions about others as a featured element in this film. How does gaining cultural competency help us to confront biased opinions based on stereotypes?
2. Explore the notion of compromise in interacting with others and in gaining cultural competency. Describe ways that you may have had to alter your viewpoints or stop resisting change in order to fit in or to accept something new.
3. Toula and Ian are learning to compromise yet will also want to hold on to their separate heritages. Discuss ways that they might do this while also creating their own family traditions.

Learning goals in the English language classroom include increasing cultural awareness and intercultural competence along with gaining language skills. Through various films that exemplify intercultural themes, students are exposed to natural language use and realistic social situations that provide opportunities to develop linguistic competence. Films offer teachers and their students' opportunities to gain understandings about how people from different cultures communicate with each other and adapt to new situations. Rich discussions inspired by the three films suggested here can lead students into critical explorations and meaningful writing experiences around issues like ethnocentrism, discrimination, stereotypes and acculturation. They provide provocative and compelling examples that may not be "real-life" but that students can relate to and connect to emotionally. Lastly, films can contribute to the goal of intercultural competence by helping learners see the world from another perspective and to develop empathy, understanding, openness and interest in other persons and cultures.

Conclusion

This chapter tried to show that the use of cross-cultural films in English language classrooms has the potential of developing students' knowledge and skills in intercultural communication. While it must be noted that every viewing, listening, and reading must incorporate activating one's critical thinking skills, it must also be kept in mind that while a cultural value may be visible in one movie, other aspects of the movie may contain inaccurate perceptions (Jandt, 2018). As Byram (1997) articulates, often times, "the stories told are prejudiced and stereotyped, particularly in processes of informal socialisation, within the family or in the media, for example" (p. 36). Therefore, except for very short pieces from movies that are used in in classrooms for instructive purposes, all viewing activities must be accompanied by critical thinking and problem-solving skills that can facilitate students' learning of cultural issues without creating stereotypes.

References

Byram, M. (1997). *Teaching and assessing intercultural communicative competence.* Clevedon: Multilingual.

Jandt, F. E. (2018). *An introduction to intercultural communication: Identities in a global community* (9th ed.). Thousand Oaks, CA: Sage.

Marks, L. U. (2000). *The skin of the film: Intercultural cinema, embodiment, and the senses.* Durham: Duke University Press.

Nur, S. (2014). Increasing students' cultural awareness by using film in teaching cross cultural understanding. *The 61st TEFLIN International Conference,* UNS Solo 2014.

Roell, C. (2010). Intercultural training with films. *English Teaching Forum,* 48(2), 2–15.

Stringer, D. M., & Cassidy, P. A. (2009). *52 Activities for improving cross-cultural communication.* Boston, MA: Intercultural Press.

Summerfield, E. (1993). *Crossing cultures through film.* Yarmouth, ME: Intercultural Press.

Film Credits

Jeffcoat, J. (Director). (2007). *Outsourced.* [Film]. Shadow Catcher Entertainment.

Shum, M. (Director). (1995). *Double happiness.* [Film]. Fine Line Features.

Zwick, J. (Director). (2002). *My big fat Greek wedding* [Film]. Gold Circle Films.

Ceylan Yangın Ersanlı and Deren Başak Akman Yeşilel

8 Raising Intercultural Awareness of Young Learners

In recent years, the emphasis on learning a foreign language at early ages has increased in all over the world. There is a considerable amount of debate on "the younger the better" quotation. Early studies indicate the existence of a "critical period" for acquisition of mother tongue but there is still not enough evidence about its existence in terms of foreign language learning. Some of the studies demonstrate that older learners are more effective language learners when compared to the younger ones (Marinova-Todd, Marshall, and Snow, 2000; Ur, 2001). On the other hand, there are other studies proving the advantages of starting a foreign language learning at early ages (Cameron, 2001; Read, 2003; Ersöz, 2007; Dewaele, 2014; Larsen-Hall, 2008; Shin and Crandall, 2014). Dewaele (2014) stated that UK Secretary of State for Education changed the policy in 2002. Compulsory modern foreign language course was offered to 14- to 16-year-olds before, but later, by changing the policy, those courses have been introduced in primary schools believing that starting at a younger age is the best way of making pupils enjoy and feel confident about speaking another language and culture other than their own. Ersöz (2007) claims that since children have less barriers – biological, social, emotional, neurological – learning a foreign language comes closer to acquisition. She adds that learning a foreign language at younger ages is beneficial because children can develop a lifelong ability to communicate with more people; become more creative and better problem solvers; can understand their own culture deeply and learn to respect other cultures and may have better job opportunities in the future. There are still other studies that point out not age but conditions matter (Rixon, 1999). According to Read (2003, p. 7) starting to learn a foreign language is better when learning is:

- Natural
- Contextualized and part of a real event
- Interesting and enjoyable
- Relevant
- Social
- Purposeful for the child
- Builds on things the child knows
- Multi-sensory

- A part of a coherent whole
- Active and experiential
- Challenging
- Supported appropriately

Who Are Young Learners?

In the literature, it is stated that the term "young learners" refers to the ages between 6 to 12. Since children may start learning a foreign language before that period, they can also be included in this category. However, the young learners ages between 3–6 are generally known as "very young learners". Accepting that, especially in recent years, learning a foreign language starts before schooling age, one needs to consider physical, cognitive, social, emotional differences between a three-year-old and a twelve-year-old kid. That is to say, there is a difference between what a four-year-old can do and what an eleven-year-old can do. Taking this fact into account, Ersöz (2007) states that we need to consider four related but separate developmental areas:

Physical development: It refers to motor control. For example, a three-year-old may not hold a pencil appropriately or use scissors effectively. But as he gets older, he can control his muscles effectively.

Cognitive development: It refers to intellectual growth. The way of reaching, processing and storing the information differs as the child matures.

Socio-emotional development: This refers to growth in social behavior. As the child matures, he interacts not only with his immediate environment but with others in the society and thus becomes a social being. At younger ages, kids are often egocentric but as they grow up, they become more social and learn to cooperate.

Communicative development: This area is closely related to other developmental areas. "In order to understand the abstract nature of language, the child has to develop cognitively. In order to be able to produce speech, he has to develop physically. In order to use language and communication appropriately, he has to develop socio-emotionally" (p. 5).

Characteristics of Young Learners

Shin and Crandall (2014), Scott and Ytreberg (1990) and many other scholars assert that young learners are energetic and physically active. Therefore, teachers need to design activities that allow children move around and act out. Total

Physical Response (TPR) is commonly used with young learners as it ties language to actions.

They are spontaneous and not afraid to speak out or participate. Unlike older learners, young learners are not afraid of being judged by others. They are natural chatterboxes and are very enthusiastic. "They are good imitators of language, in part because they are not afraid to repeat after the teacher or sing along to fun songs, even if their use of the language isn't exactly right or even if they don't understand every word" (Shin and Crandall, 2014, p. 27).

Young learners are very curious and willing to discover the world around them. They are very positive about learning new things. If teachers prepare activities to increase their curiosity, they may give learners a reason to use the language they are learning. As they are receptive to new ideas, introducing different cultures can also take their attention. They like to be praised for what they did well and have the feeling of success. Therefore, it is important to praise them and keep motivated.

They are imaginative and enjoy make-believe. Role plays, drama activities allow young learners play "make-believe". Using stories also allow learners use their imagination while learning the language. Teachers can also create an imaginary world for the students and ask them to act out. They love to play and learn best when they are enjoying themselves. However, it should be kept in mind that they may sometimes have problems in differentiating fact and fiction at younger ages but later they can tell the difference. Teachers can make use this to create a fun atmosphere in the classroom.

Moreover, although they are very curious and enthusiastic, they have very short concentration and attention span. Therefore, they can be easily distracted. In young learners' classrooms, using variety of fun activities, bright colorful materials and increasing learners' curiosity is a must. Otherwise, they can easily get distracted and lose their attention. As children mature, their attention span increases.

Young learners are also known to be egocentric and relate new ideas to themselves. It is quite difficult for a child to put himself in the shoes of others and perceive the events from their perspective. Therefore, teachers need to give opportunities to personalize what they learn. For example, if the teacher uses a story or a topic from different cultures, she may let learners relate it to their own culture. They don't like to share up to age of 6 or 7. They prefer to play and work alone but in the company of others.

While they are egocentric on the one side, they are quite social on the other. As is mentioned before, young learners are quite talkative and like to play games with each other. Teachers should plan and balance different activities that require cooperation among students sometimes and individual study other times. Pair or group works are to be used to encourage interaction in the classroom.

Although they do not always understand the rules, they know that the world is governed by rules and feel secure. As they mature, they can decide on the best ways about their own learning and talk about what they like or dislike. They use language skills long before they are aware of them.

How Children Learn

Young learners do not come to class as tabula rasa. They bring a set of skills and characteristics that may help them while learning a foreign language. Taking the above mentioned characteristics into account, teachers can build on the new knowledge. Young learners have limited skills and knowledge about the target language but they still use this limited knowledge creatively. They are creative with grammar and concepts. If they do not know the exact word but have a familiar concept in their mind, they can simply produce a new word and convey their message without breaking the flow of the communication.

They have natural curiosity and enthusiasm for discovering the world around. If teachers choose right methods and techniques to be used, children are just ready to grasp the language. Although they do not understand each and every word, they are still good at interpreting the meaning. Their imagination operates at high levels. Young learners generally learn indirectly rather than directly. Teachers can design tasks without focusing on the language. While trying to complete the task, they unconsciously use the necessary language to complete the task. However, one needs to keep in mind that both direct and indirect learning are beneficial in young learners' classroom. Teachers sometimes need to use noticing activities and let students practice the language in context. They may learn from the environment (peripheral learning) as well.

Young learners learn slowly and forget easily. Therefore, repetition is very essential in their classrooms. Teachers need to trigger different senses to make learning permanent. Children are full of physical energy and need to be physically active. Such learners are known as kinesthetic learners and need action-oriented, active learning processes. Some of the learners are auditory and learn through listening. For such learners, teachers can use story telling type activities. Some other learners are visual and learn through seeing. Words are not enough for those learners. Visual materials such as pictures, flash cards, puppets, realia are suitable for them while learning. If teachers demonstrate what they want them to do, this may be very helpful to them. As learners have different learning styles, variety is a must in the classroom. Variety of activities – sometimes pair/

group work, sometimes individual study – variety of pace, variety of materials, even variety of voice. As Ersöz (2007, p. 9) states "effective teaching is possible only when the teaching style of the teachers matches with the learning styles of the majority of the students. In order to create this match, teachers should use a wide variety of materials and activities". Those activities should encourage cooperation rather than competition in the classroom.

Children learn by doing, exploring and interacting with their environment. According to Piaget, children interact with their environment and solve the problems they encounter. "It is through taking actions to solve problems that learning occurs" (in Cameron 2001, p. 2). For him, children are thinkers and active learners. He believes that children construct the knowledge on their own while solving the problems and interacting with their environment. Moreover, he claims that children have to be mature enough to undertake certain tasks. In order to complete the task, a child has to develop cognitively and this process happens in stages. Although there may be some individual differences, each and every child goes through those processes and he has to be mature enough to transit the next stage. Those stages are: sensory-motor stage where children use their senses to learn and develop their motor skills, pre-operational stage, concreate operational stage and finally formal operational stage. Young learners attending primary school fall into pre-operational and concreate operational period. At pre-operational period (2–7 years), children learn language and use words and pictures to represent objects. They are egocentric so have problems in understanding the world from others' perspective. Although they develop cognitively, they still think the world around them concretely. At concreate operational period (7–11 years) children start to think more logically. Yet they are still very concrete. They start to understand conservation concept. That is, they understand that a wide short glass and tall narrow glass have the same amount of liquid. They become less egocentric and start to understand that everybody does not necessarily think or believe in the same way they do. After the age of 11, children start to understand abstract concepts (Karatepe, 2012). Cameron (2001) states that according to Piaget, a child develops as his knowledge and thinking develops gradually and his thinking develops through actions taken to solve the problems. Action is fundamental to cognitive development. Children learn through their own actions and explorations; therefore, teachers need to bring materials from the real world that allow children to interact and discover.

Vygotsky also highlights the importance of social interaction in child's learning. Children construct knowledge by interacting with the people around who are more knowledgeable (teachers, parents, peers, etc.). Adults and language play a significant role in child's cognitive development. "Language provides the child with a new tool, opens up new opportunities for doing things and for organizing information through the use of words as symbols" (Cameron, 2001, p. 5). Adults also assist children while solving the problems on their own. This assistance is also known as "scaffolding". Adults are very important figures in child's learning in that they actively work with children in the Zone of Proximal Development (ZPD) that refers to "the difference between the child's capacity to solve problems on her/his own and her/his capacity to solve them with assistance" (Shin and Crandall, 2014, p. 34).

Through the technological development, the world gets smaller day by day. We have a chance to reach the farthest corner of the world though the internet and we have better opportunities to travel in all over the world. English is the international language and serves as the medium of communication to interact with others. Through learning a language, children learn to respect other languages and cultures. For that reason, in language classrooms it is important to use materials from different cultures in all over the world including their own culture. This may help them to understand their own culture, reflect on it and talk about it in English. This develops "what Kramsch and Sullivan (1996) call a 'sphere of interculturality' in the classroom, one that promotes a healthy process of learning about cultural differences through reflection on one's own culture" (Shin and Crandall, 2014, p. 12).

Culture and Foreign Language Education

There have been striking differences in the views of language in the past decades. The fields of second language acquisition (SLA) and foreign language education (FLE) have witnessed a shift from approaches that view language as a system to more meaning focused views. As a response to the dominance of views that focus mainly on disconnected and decontextualized units of language, communicative functions of language have begun to gain prominence in the area of language learning and teaching. The ultimate aim of the recent pedagogy is to enable language learners communicate effectively in the target language. Thus, the term "communicative competence" has emerged in 1980s. There have been many definitions and classifications of the term suggested by different scholars (Canale and Swain, 1980; Bachman, 1990; Celce-Murcia, Dornyei and Therrell, 1995). Although there has not been reached a total consensus about the components of communicative competence, the related literature suggests that grammatical, sociolinguistic, discourse and strategic competencies constitute communicative competence as a whole. However, more recently this term has come to be viewed as inadequate to equip language learners to communicate effectively with the representatives of target culture. There have been numerous studies highlighting the close relationship between culture and language (Kramsch, 1993; Lange, 2003). Languages are loaded with lots of cultural elements which link individuals to other individuals as a group. In this way language and culture are highly inter-related. Thus, scholars began to search for ways to integrate culture in language courses. Inevitably, culture studies in the fields of SLA and FLE flourished in 1980s. Especially with the advent of communicative language teaching this movement gained momentum in 1990s. Many scholars demonstrated an interest and began to view culture a fundamental and indispensable component of com-municative competence.

There are many definitions of culture given in different professions. For anthropologists and other behavioral scientists, culture is the full range of learned human behavioral patterns. Peck (1998) defines culture as the reflections of a community's agreed and modelled behaviors. However, these behavioral definitions of culture are criticized. More recent definitions of culture go a few steps further than those visible behavioral patterns to invisible aspects of it. Kramsch (1998) defines culture as a common system of standards for perceiving, believing, evaluating, and acting. Today it can be defined as the reflections of a society's agreed moral values, beliefs, judgments, ways of thinking, life philos-ophy and interpretations which distinguish them from other societies.

Attitudes of Language Teachers towards Culture Teaching

Despite the increased interest and emphasis on the teaching culture in language classrooms, for most language teachers, the teaching of target culture is not given priority (Asay et al., 2019; Castro et al., 2004; Diaz, 2013). Scholars propose some arguments for the lack of emphasis on culture:

- Teachers may be unsure about how to address cultural issues,
- Teachers may not know how to assess culture learning,
- Teachers may not want to spend limited classroom time to teach culture,
- Non-native teachers may feel themselves inadequate in teaching the target culture since they do not have enough opportunity to live in that culture,
- Some students may have negative attitudes towards target culture in the fear of losing their own cultural identity and teachers may not know how to over-come these problems.

Despite these challenges given above, culture and communication are connected to each other in such a close way that most scholars are in favor of introducing the cultural dimension as an integral part of SLA and FLE.

However, currently culture teaching has gone beyond the teaching of target culture to a more intercultural perspective. The reason behind this is the new status English has gained in the world – the *lingua franca* status. English is the most widely used language in the world today. People in all over the world speak and try to learn English for different aims. Recent studies put forward that the number of non-native speakers of English have outnumbered the native speaker ones. This means that English has become a global language. Therefore, learners of English will most probably need to communicate in English with not only the representatives of the target culture but also with the representatives of diverse cultural backgrounds. This makes it inevitable to bring an "intercultural perspective" in our language teaching practices.

Intercultural Communicative Competence (ICC)

Intercultural approach has gained a significant role in the globalized world today. Biebricher et al. (2019) claim that an intercultural approach to language teaching is necessary to help language learners develop skills they need to interact successfully with others across cultural differences. This means that individuals need to have the ability to relate with members of diverse cultural backgrounds in an effective way. To do this they will not only need to have communicative competence but also intercultural communicative competence (ICC) (Byram, 2012). The former is being able to communicate appropriately and accurately, while the latter refers to being able to engage with cultural diversities while being aware of one's own cultural identity.

Byram (1997) proposes five savoirs, the knowledge and skills needed to mediate between cultures, of ICC:

- Knowledge of self and other; of how interaction occurs; of the relationship of the individual to society.
- Knowing how to interpret and relate information.
- Knowing how to engage with the political consequences of education; being critically aware of cultural behaviors.
- Knowing how to discover cultural information.
- Knowing how to be: how to relativize oneself and value the attitudes and beliefs of the other.

As is evident from the savoirs given, ICC helps us use linguistic knowledge and cultural awareness, and be aware of our own cultural identity and others' cultures, have the skills of interpreting and relating. Fantini (2006, p. 12) defines ICC as complex abilities needed to perform effectively and appropriately when interacting with others who are linguistically and culturally different from one-self. Learners who have ICC can interpret the different interactional norms of distinct cultures in a more effective way. They are more open and tolerant to differences. However, ICC should not be limited to factual knowledge. It is more than that; it is a combination of knowledge, skills and attitudes an individual should have to communicate effectively with the representatives of other cultural backgrounds.

Relevance of Intercultural Awareness in Curriculum Development

According to the report of The Common European Framework of Reference for Languages (CEFR), intercultural awareness is a skill which should be fostered in all over Europe. It states that knowledge, awareness and the understanding of the relation (similarities and distinctive differences) between the "world of origin" and the "world of the target community" produce intercultural awareness (2001). Learners are expected to develop an awareness of a wider range of cultures than their L1. The report proposes that the role of FLE is to help learners have intercultural skills which include ICC to bring the culture of origin and foreign cultures into relation with each other.

Turkey accepts the principles of CEFR while designing the curriculum of FLE. This means that the Ministry of National Education promotes intercultural awareness and ICC in our schools. In line with this, the curriculum in our state schools involves multicultural elements which foster intercultural awareness. The methods, course books, activities and materials suggested all promote an intercultural awareness. Scholars have published many researches and given in-service trainings to language teachers about how to use an intercultural approach in a foreign language teaching and learning context. It is assumed that a teacher's role is to support the development of learners' intercultural awareness. It is stated that the best way to do this is to help them be aware of their own cultural identity and have a curiosity about other cultures. The key skill to accomplish this is "noticing" (Liddicoat, 2008). Thus, language teachers should help learners notice their own cultural norms such as values and beliefs and guide them to accomplish a curiosity for differences.

However, as discussed before many language teachers face some difficulties in promoting intercultural elements in their courses. One of the main reasons is that they are unsure about how to balance language teaching and teaching of other cultures within a limited classroom time.

Intercultural Awareness as a Lifelong Process and Young Learners

Intercultural language learning helps learners gain the necessary knowledge, skills and attitudes in engaging in interactions with the members from diverse linguistic and cultural backgrounds. While developing these skills learners who have intercultural awareness also expected to be aware of their own cultural identities. Teachers' role is like a facilitator in this process.

However, the findings of the researches on culture teaching in FLE suggest that there is mismatch between the classroom practices and what is theoretically suggested (Asay et al., 2019). It is evident that most teachers lack instructional strategies needed to teach culture. It should be noted that gaining intercultural awareness is a long process. Kolb (1984) states that it is acquired through a lifelong learning process and is best developed through conscious, planned and facilitated experiential learning (cited in Briga, 2019). Similarly, Lomicka (2009) claims that intercultural awareness is achieved over time. As discussed before, intercultural awareness involves identity formation, being open and tolerant to new cultures, ways of lives, beliefs and judgments. Therefore, the best starting point in the development of an intercultural awareness should be the early ages. However, there is little empirical research in particular on the development of intercultural awareness in young learners (Sharpe, 2001; Moloney, 2009). With the rapid spread of English as a global language and the increase in the intercultural interactions, early language instruction has gained prominence in many countries. Therefore, it is high time to examine how intercultural awareness of young learners can be developed.

The intercultural materials, and activities should be appropriate to cognitive, psychological, linguistic and physical developmental levels of young learners. Experiential learning should be supported. Limited classroom time may not be enough to develop an intercultural awareness in learners. The process should be supported by learners' daily lives. Non-formal education has also a definite effect on their intercultural awareness. Thus, teachers should foster learner autonomy, and give real life tasks which help learners go on developing themselves outside the classroom without the actual presence of the teacher.

Sample Lesson Plan

Name of activity: Grandma Went to the Market **Skills and language exponents:** Listening, Speaking, Vocabulary, writing **Topic:** intercultural awareness

Material: World map, color pencils **Number of learners:** 20 **Grade & Age of learners:** Grade 5 & 11 **Interaction:** Teacher-student, student –student (pair work and group work) **Language level:** A2 **Time:** 40 minutes **Learning outcomes:** At the end of the activity the students will have insights into some artefacts about their own culture and other cultures.	
Warm-up	**Procedure:** 1. The teacher asks what can people/tourists buy in Turkey? What is a typical souvenir? S/he tries to elicit "carpet". 2. The teacher points to the map on the board. S/he points to countries Thailand, Mexico, China, Switzerland, Kenya, Russia, Japan, Australia, Peru. 3. S/he asks what would they like to buy/get from these countries? S/he elicits answers, accepts all answers from students. 4. The teacher introduces vocabulary with pictures. *Carpet* *Cats* *Masks* *Cowbells* *Lanterns* *Drums* *Nesting dolls* *Boomerangs* *Kites* *Llamas*
	5. The teacher wants the students to predict which country they can buy/get these above. Then s/he introduces the story. She wants them to listen and watch the story.
While listening	**Procedure:** 1. The teacher makes the students listen & watch the story on the following link: https://www.youtube.com/watch?v=1rWUIwJpMdg 2. She asks questions about gist on first listening: *What does Grandma do? How does she travel?* 3. The teacher asks students to check their predictions and match items and countries on second listening. 4. The teacher checks answers with the whole class.

Follow-up	**Procedure:** 1. The teacher asks students to form small groups (of three or four) 2. S/he distributes sheets of paper with world map on it. The students brainstorm what countries they would like to visit. 3. Then students individually mark the countries they would like to visit and draw what they would like to buy from there. 4. The teacher models speaking with one of the students: *Where would you like to go? What would you like to buy?* 5. The students practice the interaction in pairs.
Homework	Students prepare a poster or collage on a world map after further internet research. They write 5 to 10 sentences about their travel. The posters are displayed in the classroom.

References

Asay, T. D., Martinsen, A. R., Bateman, E. B., & Erickson, G. R. 2019. A survey of teachers' integration of culture in secondary foreign language classrooms. *The NECTFL Review*, 83, 9-39.

Bachman, L. 1990. *Fundamental considerations in language testing*. Oxford: Oxford University Press. ISBN 978-0-19-437003-5.

Biebricher, C., East, M., Howard, J., & Tolosa, C. 2019. Navigating intercultural teaching in New Zeland classrooms. *Cambridge Journal of Education*, 49(5), 605-621. https://doi.org/10.1080/0305764X.2019.1581137

Briga, E. 2019. Intercultural learning for pupils and teachers: A good practice case study from an Erasmus+ project. In M. Kowalczuk-Waledziak et al. (Eds.), *Rethinking teacher education for the 21st century* (pp. 329–339). Opladen:Verlag Barbara Budrich.

Byram, M. 1997. *Teaching and assessing intercultural communicative competence*. Clevedon, England: Multilingual Matters.

Byram, M. 2012. Language awareness and (critical) cultural awareness— Relationships, comparisons and contrasts. *Language Awareness*, 21(1–2), 5-13.

Cameron, L. 2001. *Teaching languages to young learners*. Cambridge: Cambridge University Press.

Canale, M., & Swain, M. 1980. Theoretical bases of communicative approaches to second language teaching and testing. *Applied Linguistics*, 1, 1-47. http://dx.doi.org/10.1093/applin/I.1.1

Castro, P., Sercu, L., & Garcia, M. C. M. 2004. Integrating language and culture teaching: An investigation of Spanish teachers' perceptions of the objectives of foreign language education. *Intercultural Education*, 15(1), 91–104.

CEFR (2001). *Common European Framework of Reference for Languages: Learning, Teaching, Assessment*. Strasbourg: Council of Europe. https://rm.coe.int/1680459f97 Prevention 41–45.

Celce-Murcia, M., Dornyei, Z., & Thurrell, S. 1995. Communicative competence: A pedagogically motivated model with content specifications. *Issues in Applied Linguistics*, 6(2). Retrieved from https://escholarship.org/uc/item/2928w4zj.

Dewaele, J. 2014. Why "younger" is not always "better" in foreign language learning. http://blogs.bbk.ac.uk/research/2014/10/08/why-younger-is-not-always-better-in-foreign-language-learning/.

Diaz, A. 2013. Intercultural understanding and professional learning through critical engagement. *Babel*, 48(1), 12-19.

Ersöz, A. 2007. *Teaching English to young learners*. Ankara: EDM.

Fantini, A. E. 2006. Exploring and assessing intercultural competence. Retrieved May 1, 2007, from http://www.sit.edu/publications/docs/feil_research_report.pdf.

Karatepe, Ç. 2012. Learning theories. In Gürsoy, E. & Arıkan, A. (Eds.), *Teaching English to young learners: An activity-based guide for prospective teachers*. Ankara: Eğiten Kitap.

Kramsch, C. 1993. *Context and culture in language teaching*. Oxford: Oxford University Press.

Kramsch, C. 1998. *Language and culture*. Oxford: Oxford University Press.

Lasen-Hall, J. 2008. Weighing the benefits of studying a foreign language at a younger starting age in a minimal input situation. *Second Language Research*, 24(1), 35–63. https://doi.org/10.1177/0267658307082981

Liddicoat, A. J. 2008. Language choices in the intercultural language classroom. *Babel*, 43(1), 18-35.

Lomicka, L. L. May 2009. An intercultural approach to teaching and learning French. *The French Review*, 82(6), 1227.

Marinova-Todd, S. H., Marshall, D. B., & Snow, C. E. 2000. Three misconceptions about age and L2 learning. *TESOL Quarterly*, 34(1), 9-34.

Moloney, R. 2009. Forty per cent French: Intercultural competence and identity in an Australian language classroom. *Intercultural Education*, 20(1), 71-81. https://doi.org/10.1080/14675980802700854

Peck, D. 1998. *Teaching culture: Beyond language*. Yale: New Haven Teachers Institute.

Read, C. 2003. Is younger better? English Teaching Professional https://www.
carolread.com/publications/book-chapters-and-articles/.

Rixon, S. 1999. *Young learners of English: Some research perspectives.*
Harlow: Longman.

Scott, W. A., & Ytreberg, L. H. 1990. *Teaching English to children.*
New York: Longman.

Shin, J. K., & Crandall, J. 2014. *Teaching young learners English: From theory to
practice.* Boston: Heinle- National Geographic Learning.

Ur, P. (2001). Check it out. *Language Teaching Professional.* In D. L. Lange
& R. M. Paige (Eds.), *Culture as the core: Perspectives on culture in second
language learning* (pp. 173–236). USA: Information Age Publishing.

Bengü Börkan

9 Classroom Assessment of L2 Cultural Knowledge

In every classroom, a teacher makes various instructional decisions such as about what learning materials should be used, whether students ready to move on to the next learning episode, what else students need, how we group students, what topics need to be reviewed, and what extent learning objectives are achieved; most of these decisions are among teachers' daily routines. In order to make these decisions sound teachers should be skilled at collecting data or information about their students. Airasian (1991) define classroom assessment as a process of obtaining information for making an instructional decision in an attempt to improve teaching and learning (Airasian, 1991). This chapter introduces various assessment techniques and approaches playing the important role in instruction and learning in the assessment of intercultural communication competence.

Basic Terms: Assessment, Test, Measurement, and Evaluation

Assessment, a test, measurement, and evaluation frequently used terms in classroom assessment jargon might be used interchangeably by teachers. *Assessment* is the broadest term among them and can be defined as a process of collecting information to make decision about learning. In this process, various instruments including a test were used to collect systematic information. *A test* is defined as an instrument including tasks that have students to display their performance in written, physically or verbally. *Measurement* is defined as a process of obtaining a value (usually a score) that shows the degree to which a specified attribute is exist according to some rules. *Evaluation* is a process of making a value judgment about merit, worth and significance of students' performance (Nitko & Brookhart, 2007).

Formative and Summative Assessment

Instructional decisions could be for purely formative or purely summative purposes, or for any purposes between these two extremes. Assessments become formative if the information obtained through assessment tasks are used to modify teaching and learning activities to meet student needs (Black, Harrison,

Lee, Marshall, & William, 2004). Feedback is a key element in formative assessment, which should be used to close the gap between the actual and the reference level of a performance (Ramaprasad, 1983; Sadler, 1989). However, summative assessment is undertaken at a particular point in time, such as after completion of instruction to generate a grade that reflects the student's achievement (Nitko & Brookhart, 2007). Summative assessment does not have direct effect on teaching and learning. However, information obtained through summative assessment could have been used to make decisions which may have high stake consequences for the student (Sadler, 1989).

Assessment Techniques

Various assessment techniques are means of eliciting students' behavior to measure their level of ability, achievement or skills. Researchers have different approaches to address these assessment techniques, in this section assessment techniques will be discussed in three main groups; (1) selected response items, (2) constructed response items and (3) performance items.

Selected Response Items

Selected response items require students to select a correct answer or best answer from the list of alternatives (options) given in the items. True-false items, multiple-choice items and matched items are types of selected response items.

True-False Items

A true-false item consists of a stem (a statement or a proposition) and two mutually exclusive alternatives, true and false. Although true and false are commonly used two alternatives, other labels can be used as well depending on form of a statement, proposition or question in the item stem. Yes-no, right-wrong and fact-opinion are some examples for dichotomous response alternatives.

An example:

Assessments become formative if information obtained through assessment are used to modify teaching and learning activities to meet student needs.	True False
German university students knock on the table instead of clapping after a speech or presentation.	Fact Opinion

Among three types of selected response item, true-false items are criticized the most. Teachers often use this item type because it is relatively easy to write, easy to score, an objective and wide range of learning objectives can be covered in one test with true-false items. On the other hand, teachers often poorly construct items that only assess simple facts and knowledge and such items encourage students to study factual details. Students are having difficult time in understanding what is asked in true-false items when statements are copied from the course materials because they have been taken out of their context (Nitko & Brookhart, 2007). Moreover, the odds of blindly guessing the correct alternatives is 50 percent. Suggestions for increasing quality of true-false items are given below.

Guidelines for writing true-false items

1. The item assesses an important learning objective.
2. The statement is brief and have simple language.
3. The statements do not have double negatives.
4. The statement has negative statements if really necessary.
5. The statement is free from verbal clues/specific determiners (e.g., always, never, may).
6. The statement is unequivocally judged true or false.
7. The statement barrowed from course materials is paraphrased.
8. Length of statements are about the same.
9. The correct options are not patterned or repeat itself (e.g. TFTFTFTF or FFFFFTF)

Sax (1997) offered strategies to minimize chance factor in true-false items. The test score is corrected by using the following formula. The corrected score is obtained by subtracting the number of wrong answers from the number of right ones.

$$S_{CG} = R - \frac{\#\ of\ wrong\ items}{\#\ of\ options - 1}$$

Commonly used another strategy to reduce the effect guessing is to have students correct any item marked false. Although this format offers more information about student understanding, teachers need to trade of between reducing the effect of guessing, and advantage of easy scoring in true-false items. Because the format of the true-false item gets closer to the format of a short-answer item with this strategy, the number of items in the test gets reduced for the same length of time.

Multiple True-False Items

The multiple true-false item, with some characteristics of the true-false and the multiple-choice items, is an efficient way of testing examinee knowledge about complex phenomena (Albanese & Sabers, 1988). It has a stem as the true-false item does and multiple options as the multiple-choice item does. In this item type, students need to mark every right option. Hancock, Thiede, Sax, and Michael (1993) indicate that the multiple true-false item provides a significantly more reliable measure than the true-false item.

An example:

"As you will learn in this test, there are multiple approaches to measuring any given construct. Consider the example of academic achievement. A student's achievement in a specific area can be measured using a number of different approaches. For example, a teacher might base a student's grade in a course on a variety of components including traditional paper-and-pencil tests (e.g., multiple-choice, short-answer, and essay items), homework assignments, class projects, performance assessments, and portfolios. Although all of these different approaches typically are aimed at measuring the knowledge, skills, and abilities of students, each had its own unique characteristics". (Reynolds, Livingston, & Wilson, 2006, p. 10)

What can be said based on the paragraph given above, select all that are true

* 1) Multiple-choice items are traditional paper-and-pencil tests
  2) Performance assessment compared to other techniques has unique characteristics
*3) There can be more than one way to measure the same construct
  4) A teacher should base a student's course grade on multiple measures

* correct statements

Multiple Choice Items

The multiple-choice item consists of an introductory material and/or question and a list of two or more alternatives. The item stem usually includes the task (e.g. paragraph, picture, graph, problem, and data) and presents what students are expected to perform.

An example:

"Thirty years ago, perhaps, but today Shinobu is anything but ordinary. The proper Japanese meal, prepared by the mother and eaten on the tatami mat by the entire family, is increasingly rare, thanks to long hours at work and at school, and social changes that have resulted in more women working out of the home and delaying marriage. With limited time and inclination for balanced home cooking, many people simply grab prepackaged meals at ubiquitous convenience stores, or down fattening fast food. That has nutritionists and public officials fearing that knowledge of traditional Japanese cooking—and eating—is being lost. 'I think we're in a crisis situation now,' says Nobuo Harada, a food expert at Kokushikan University outside Tokyo. 'We're in the process of losing the food culture of Japan.'"

The paragraph above was excerpted from an article titled 'Lamenting the Decline of the Home-Cooked Meal in Japan' in https://time.com/.

In his paragraph what elements of culture are NOT exemplified?
A) Language
B) Symbol
C) Value
D) Norm

Matching Items

A matching item includes a list of premises and a list of options. Student is required to match each premise with one of the responses. Premises consist of words, definitions, parts of sentences and pictures.

An example:

Directions: In the left column below national holidays around the world are given. For each description of holiday, choose the name of the holiday. Each name in the right column may be used once, more than once, or not at all.

Characteristics of national holidays	Name of celebration
____ 1) Held annually in Munich, Bavaria, Germany	a) Nowruz
____ 2) Children's festivals take place throughout Turkey, held on April 23 each year.	b) National Sovereignty and Children's Day

____ 3) The Persian New Year	c) Oktoberfest
____ 4) Cultural and religious celebration held on 17 March in Ireland and Irish diaspora	d) Halloween
____ 5) This French national holiday is celebrated on July 14	e) Saint Patrick's Day
	f) Bastille Day

The matching item is similar to the multiple-choice test and relatively easier to construct. Compare to the true-false item, it has lower chance factor. However, unless it is well constructed, most matching items measures memorization

Guidelines for matching items

1. The item assesses an important learning objective.
2. Premises and responses are homogeneous.
3. Item has directions explaining the basis of matching.
4. There are fewer than 10 responses.
5. Number of responses are more than number of premises in the list.
6. Statements in premises are longer than in responses.
7. If possible, responses are ordered in a meaningful way.

Constructed Response Item

Constructed response items involve completion, short answer and essay items.

Completion and Short Answer

Completion and short answer are similar items with only minor distinction between them. *Completion item* consists of sentence or paragraph with at least one missing word and requires a student supplies the missing words. Completion item is also known as the fill in the blank item. *Short answer item* requires student type a word, phrase, number, a full sentence as a response.

Examples:

Item Type
Completion   _____ is a traditional Moroccan house or palace with an interior garden or courtyard.
The cities of Fez, Meknes, Marrakesh and Rabat are collectively known as _____.

Short answer	List three things that are rude to a Japanese but not to you? What are the dominant religious in Japan? Who are the major ethnic minorities in Japan?

Essay Items

The last type of a constructed response item is an essay item. There are two distinct uses of an essay item: (1) measuring achievement and (2) measuring writing ability. Teachers use this item type to measure students' achievement in many courses such as social studies and science. In second language courses an essay item is used to measure student's writing ability (Hopkins, 1998). It is beyond the scope of this chapter to cover an assessment of writing ability.

In assessing achievement, an essay item differs from a short-answer item in that students' responses are extensive and detailed. In short-answer item, students answer is very restricted and usually an answer involves a few words. It usually requires students to recall some knowledge or fact. On the other hand, student's answer to an essay item is less structured. An item sometimes does not have absolute single answer and it is meant to measure some cognitive skills more than simple recall. An example of an essay item to measure achievement:

> Watch the movie "My Big Fat Greek Wedding". Through the actions of the characters, analyze what the film indicates about the cultural patterns of Greeks. Discuss the similarities and differences with your own culture.

An essay item is less objective than other items types mentioned so far in this chapter. Therefore, it calls for sensitive and thoughtful scoring procedure. Here some suggestions for scoring essay items to increase the objectivity of the test results.

Guidelines for scoring an essay item

1. The scoring procedure should be planned while constructing essay item.
2. Remove or cover names on papers before starting scoring.
3. If there is more than one items, score the same item across all papers, then, move to the next item.
4. Do not look at score of previously scored items if there is more than one item exist on the exam.
5. The essay item is read by more than one teacher, or if only one rater is possible essays will be reread by the same teacher.

Tab. 1: A Process and Product in a Performance Assessment

Course	Process	Product
Reading	Reading aloud	Picturing the story
Social sciences	Debate	Term paper- Alternative & Renewable Energy'
Physical education	Athletic performance	Term paper – living a healthy life style
Language	Presentation skills	Persuasive essay
Science	Use of a compound microscope	Lab report

Performance Assessment

In a performance assessment, a student is expected to display a performance or construct a response to elicit level of his/her achievement, competence and skill. In some school subjects a student displays a performance by answering a short-answer item, develop solution, complete research paper, or writing an essay; in other subjects by playing block flute or doing a lab experiment. However, a constructed response item such as short answer or essay usually is not considered a performance assessment. Since assessment methods (different item types) exist along a continuum of how much construction is required, it is not easy to categorize assessment types. Brookhart (2015) clearly distinguishes a performance assessment from other types of assessment by the following definition:

> A performance assessment is one that (a) require students to create a product or demonstrate a process, or both, and (b) uses observation and judgment based on clearly defined criteria to evaluate the qualities of student work. (p. 3)

With this definition in mind, any essay test measuring writing skills in language classes can be considered a type of performance assessment in which a student is required to produce a written product by using their writing skills. Likewise, a speaking test in a second language class can be considered another type of performance assessment in which teachers assess student's speaking skills by observing.

Performance assessments consist of two components; a performance task and a grading procedure (McMillan, 2007). A performance task is any activity that elicit students' level of knowledge, understanding or competence level. Performance tasks require a student produce a tangible product and/or display a performance that serve as evidence of learning. Tab. 1 provides examples for a product and process being evaluated in performance assessments.

Example:

> You need to find a busy public place where people interact (such as bus stations, post office or a bank) and where you can observe people for at least one hour or so. While observing people, take time to consider: How do they move around? What body position and movement they have? What gestures do they use? How do they interact with each other? What are the expectations for space and privacy? What emotions are expressed?
>
> Within the frame of your observation, identify and describe your own culture using an intercultural model.

Example:

> History, values, politics, economy, beliefs, and practices are the major elements of the culture. Select one country and prepare a poster to introduce this country to your classmate.

Popham (2011) listed seven important factors to consider while selecting an existing task or creating a new task in performance assessment; Generalizability, authenticity, multiple foci, teachability, fairness, feasibility and scorability. The high-quality task allows to generalize students' performance on the task to a comparable task. An authentic task is desirable, that is, the assessment should include a task similar to real word problems. The task should allow teachers to measure multiple learning objectives. In performance assessment, the task should be feasible, that is, the task should meet time, cost, space and resources constrains. The task can be scorable, that is, expected students' performance and product can be observable and evaluated reliably and accurately. A task in which students' performances and products can be observed and evaluated reliably and accurately can be scored. The last, the task should be fair to every student. The task should allow equal opportunity for students to demonstrate what they know and are capable of.

Checklists and Rating Scales

Upon the completion of the task, a process and/or a product is evaluated by using a grading procedure. The performance evaluation based on teachers' impressions and judgments is inherently subjective. Therefore, a grading procedure with well-defined evaluation criteria is needed to make an evaluation process as objective as possible. A checklist, a rating scale and a rubric guide educator how to evaluate/grade a student's performance against a set of criteria. A checklist is a list of behaviors, traits or characteristics (criteria) that teachers decide if they are either present or absent in student's performance. The checklist

Fig. 1: Example Check List for a Country Poster

Criteria	Present
History of a country is complete and accurate	☐
Unique values of a country are addressed	☐
Topics are considered impolite or taboo are given	☐
Interesting facts about a country are given	☐
Pictures and graphics are clear and relevant	☐
The poster has a nice organization and easy to follow	☐
The poster is free from spelling-grammar mistakes	☐

Fig. 2: Example Rating Scale for a Country Poster

Criteria	4 Satisfactory	3 Acceptable	2 Needs improvement	1 Unacceptable
History of a country				
Unique values of a country				
Impolite or taboo topics				
Interesting facts				
Pictures and graphics				
Poster organization				
Mechanics (spelling and ideas)				

is the simple form of scoring tool. Teachers observed the presence of certain behaviors, not the quality. Fig. 1 is an example of rating scale which is developed for a country poster.

Another scoring tool, a rating scale, includes criteria and rating scale with either frequency or quality ratings. Every level of rating scale (anchor points) is labeled with a quantitative value and/or a description. In the following example, both quantitative values and description are used for anchor points. Fig. 2 is an example of a rating scale. It includes the same criteria as the checklist given above and it requires teachers to evaluate students' work along a four-point quality rating scale.

The number of anchor points on the scale can vary. Checklist is a special case of rating scale with two anchor points. The more the number of anchor points is, the better an assessment differentiates among students based on how much they have skill or knowledge being tested.

Here are some examples of anchor labels:

<u>Quality rating scale</u>

Three anchor points:	*Needs improvement, meets expectations, exceed expectations*
	Intermediate, advanced, superior
Four anchor points:	*Distinguished, proficient, developing, beginning*
	Above expectations, demonstrates clear understanding, demonstrates some understanding, not satisfactory

<u>Frequency rating scale</u>

Four anchor points:	*Consistently, often, sometimes, rarely*
Five anchor points:	*Always, frequently, occasionally, seldom, never,*

Brookhart (2013) strongly recommends the careful use of checklists and rating scales. She suggests teacher to use checklists to communicate with student on instructions how to complete a task such as an assignment and a project, or on formatting requirements for an assignment. She suggests teachers to use frequency rating scale, but not quality rating scale to assess performance skills such as presentation skills and student's behaviors such as work habits. She states

> Checklists and rating scales are great when you don't need descriptions of performance quality, but rather just need to know whether something has been done (checklist) or how often or how well it has been done (rating scale). (p. 76)

Rubrics

Each anchor points in the quality rating scale refers to a performance level. However, expected student performance for each performance level is not defined in the rating scale. Teachers' or judges' opinion about these performance levels may vary. An acceptable poster based on its organization for a teacher may not be acceptable for another teacher. For higher quality measurement, these performance level needs to be clearly described. The scoring tool in which each

Fig. 3: An Example of an Analytical Rubric – a Country Poster

Criteria	4	3	2	1
Interesting facts	Catchy interesting facts are given, facts are unique to the country and important for country's culture.	Main facts are given with explanation but they are not link to countries culture.	Few facts are given but they are superficial.	No facts about a country is given.
Poster organization	The poster has an excellent design and layout. Easy to follow	Attempts to organize ideas, but better transitional language is needed. Attempt at introduction and conclusion	Lack of structure, disorganized, hard to follow, unclear introduction and conclusion	Design is very week, sections are not identifiable
Mechanics (spelling and ideas)	Spelling and grammar reflect careful editing.	Occasional errors, but they do not distract.	Frequent Mechanical errors but do not interfere with understanding.	Distracting mechanical errors throughout, blocking readability

performance level describes what a student is expected to achieve for each criterion is called an analytical rubric. Fig. 3 is an example of an analytical rubric. Instead of evaluating each criterion separately, a teacher prefers to make an overall judgment about the students' performance by considering all of the criteria simultaneously. The following rubric – a holistic rubric – describes the criteria used to categorize students' poster into a four-specific level of performance from unacceptable to satisfactory. The number of levels and the description of each level may vary depending on expectations for students' performance. Fig. 4 is an example of holistic rubric. It holds the same criteria as the analytical rubrics but a student is assigned the one of the four level best describing his or her performance (Airasian & Russell, 2008). Brookhart (2013) lists the advantage and disadvantages for analytical and holistic rubrics; for teaching purposes, analytical rubrics are better. It eases communication between students and teacher before, during and after assessment. It is helpful for feedback purposes. On the other hand, holistic rubrics are better if the sole purpose of the assessment is to assign a score to students and students do not involve actively in assessment. Scoring can be easier with holistic rubric and produce higher inter-rater reliability.

Fig. 4: An Example of a Holistic Rubric

Satisfactory	Catchy interesting facts are given, facts are unique to the country and important for country's culture. The poster has an excellent design and layout. Easy to follow. Spelling and grammar reflect careful editing.
Acceptable	Main facts are given with explanation but they are not link to countries culture. Attempts to organize ideas, but better transitional language is needed. Attempt at introduction and conclusion. Occasional errors, but they do not distract.
Needs Improvement	Few facts are given but they are superficial. Lack of structure, disorganized, hard to follow, unclear introduction and conclusion. Frequent Mechanical errors but do not interfere with understanding.
Unacceptable	No facts about a country is given. Design is very week, sections are not identifiable. Distracting mechanical errors throughout, blocking readability.

Alternative Assessment

Alternative assessment and authentic assessment are sometimes used inter-changeably with performance assessment (McMillian, 2007). Although they all have in common, they actually mean something different. An alternative assessment refers to assessment methods other than traditional techniques – selected and contracted response items. The performance assessment is an alternative assessment in this sense. Other examples of alternative assessments can be portfolio, self-assessment, and peer assessment. Authentic assessments require student use knowledge and skills to perform a task tied to real-world contexts. Some performance assessment tasks require students to display what they can do in actual world situations. In fact, authentic tasks are desirable in a performance assessment.

Portfolio

Portfolio is defined as a purposeful collection of student work that document progress, and achievement. Beyond this simple definition, portfolio is detailed depending on the purpose of use and takes different names such as writing port-folio and best work portfolio. Portfolio can be considered as a communication tool rather than assessment techniques or method because the portfolio basi-cally contains products produced by a student for performance evaluation. What is differently done in portfolio is (1) promoting metacognition through stu-dent self-assessment and reflection, and (2) highlighting student participation in selecting portfolio content with predetermined guidelines (Arter & Spandel, 1992). Portfolios do not contain haphazard, random, unrelated collections of a student work. The purpose of portfolio should be clarified first and then, there should be clear reason why certain works would be included. The content of a portfolio should be closely related to important learning objectives and each entry should reflect student's achievement and progress in the class (Airasian & Russel, 2008; Belgrad, 2013; McMillian, 2007).

The content of portfolio consists of student's products (an entry), student's self-evaluation, teacher evaluations and feedbacks. Possible entries for language art classes could be student journals, book reports, writing samples, the first and the second and the final draft of essay, and video record of reading (McMillian, 2007). The content of a portfolio depends on mainly on learning objective and then the purpose of its use. There are various types of portfolio to serve different purposes. The *growth portfolio* displays the growth (learning) of students over time. Like formative assessment, growth portfolio is used to enhance learning. The *evaluation portfolio* is used to assess student learning on specific learning objectives like summative assessment, therefore it is more standardized compared to the growth portfolio and the content is mostly determined by teacher. The *showcase portfolio* also known as the best work portfolio includes artifacts that a student selects to show his/her best work, achievement and talent. This type of portfolio is less standardized than the other two portfolio types because students decide their own artifacts and the content best reflecting their own accomplishment (Belgrad, 2013; McMillian, 2007). Although the emphases of self-evaluation and self-reflection vary across different portfolio types, they are the most important characteristics of the portfolio. Belgrad (2013) argue that:

> The purposeful design of portfolios supports reflective process of selection, self-assessment and goal setting that can lead to increased student voice and motivation and help students take responsibility for their own learning. (p. 335)

Examine the following self-reflection questions and sample portfolio entries in Fig. 5.

Why did you select this particular piece?
What do you see as the special strengths of this paper?
What would you do differently if you had a chance to do it over?
What have you learned about stereotype from your work?
What kind of writing would you like to do in the future?
How did your writing change from first draft to final draft?
Why do you think this is your best work?

Fig. 5: An Example of Portfolio Entries

Stories about memorable intercultural encounters that a student has experience

Reflective essays on stories about memorable intercultural encounters that a student has experience.

Reflective essay on a classroom discussion.

Critical analysis of a movie on student's own culture.

Student's observation of people at a coffee house.

Interview with peers from different culture.

Formative Assessment Strategies

Assessments become formative if information obtained through assessment are used to modify teaching and learning activities to meet student needs (Black, Harrison, Lee, Marshall, & William, 2004). Affective formative assessment strategies increase student achievement not only in the classrooms but also in large scale testing (McMillian, 2007). It is a common misconception that formative assessment is a set of special techniques that teachers needs to learn, and that is a special program that teachers adopt and add to what they have already done in their classroom. In fact, formative assessment is a teaching and learning philosophy in which students were assessed to inform learning and, is a learning process that teachers interact with their students to gather information to improve achievement. It is not a prepackaged program or set of techniques that teachers adopt and implement (Moss & Brookhart, 2009). For effective formative assessment, teachers need a mind shift rather than learning assessment strategies.

Hattie and Timperley (2007) suggest three questions to guide formative assessment process.

- Where am I going?
- Where am I now?
- Where to next?

These three questions need to be answered by teachers and students together in formative assessment. Teachers begin the formative assessment process by sharing learning objectives with their students and having students understand where they need to reach by the end of unite or an activity. Then, teachers quickly assess students' understanding of the content and enable student to evaluate themselves during teaching and learning activity. Finally, teachers guide students to close the gap between where they are currently and where they should be. Formative assessment covers a learning process from the beginning to the end of a learning episode. Learning episode can be a course, unite or an activity. During a formative assessment, assessment techniques covered in this chapter could be used to gather information. However, many of decisions teachers made are fast paced, so require quick assessment strategies. The following assessment strategies based upon the assessment techniques such as true-false and short-answer items can be used in formative assessment:

True/false items: The teacher direct true/false items to the whole classroom and students answer items by raising a hand or some other kind of physical response such as yes/no cards, thumbs-up/thumps-down. These days some schools prefer electronic applications for the same purpose.

Multiple cards: The teacher directs multiple-choice item to the whole classroom and students answer items by raising cards indicating the correct alternatives. Cards can be lettered and colored for each option.

Whiteboards: The teacher directs short answer or completion items to the whole classroom and students write the answer on individual small whiteboard and rise it as the teacher can see it.

Exit cards: Just before leaving class, the teacher poses a set of items (mostly sort answer items) to the whole class and have student write their answers on a card. Student will pass in before they leave class. Exit cards could be anonymous and they can be applied in an electronic medium as well.

(Informal) Observation: The teacher observes students in the classroom while students are engaging in an activity such as a problem solving and experiment.

These quick strategies which are informal assessments enable teachers to quickly assess students' understanding of the content. Strategies are not limited with those. Teachers can easily develop their own strategies to monitor their student's understanding by integrating them with their teaching activities.

Student Self-Assessment

Self-assessment is a process that helps students reflect on their own learning to create meaningful learning experiences. Through self-assessment "... students review their own work and identify strengths and weaknesses for the purpose of improving performance." (Moss & Brookhart, 2009, p. 80). McMillian (2007) emphases that "The goal of self-assessment is to empower students so that they can guide their own learning and internalize the criteria for judging success". (p. 144)

3 things you didn't know before
2 things that surprised you about the topic
1 thing you want to start doing with what you've learned

What do you know already?
What did you learn?
What do you want to know?

Some metacognitive strategies can be used to help students gain self-assessment skills. For instance, after completion of a learning activity, teachers make student answer following three questions[1]:
In a slightly different version of this activity, teachers make students answer following three questions:
In another metacognitive activity known as '321 RIQ', upon the completion of learning episode or course work, students have made a short essay that reflect three facts they recall from the course work, two insides they gained, and one question they need an answer for.

Besides metacognitive activities, checklists, rating scales, rubrics and any structured materials can be helpful to student for self-assessment (Brown & Harris, 2013). Fig. 6 is an example of self-assessment rating scale.
Other quick fairly common self-evaluation strategies in formative assessment are:

"Most clear" and "least clear" cards (Moss & Brookhart, 2009). At the end of lesson or activity, students identify the most and least clear points. Another variation includes "one thing I'm sure I know" or "one thing I'd like to know more about."

Traffic lights: Students indicate their understanding or confidence about the topic by using red, yellow and green circles. Red: I need help, Yellow: I am getting there, Green: I can do this. Students can show how they feel in various ways: cards with happy –sad faces, use thumps –up and down.

Measuring Affective Traits

An affective trait is an emotional disposition that are different from knowledge and skill and "set the threshold for the occurrence of particular emotional states"

---

1   https://www.nwea.org/blog/2019/27-easy-formative-assessment-strategies-for-gathering-evidence-of-student-learning/?.

Fig. 6: Self-Assessment Rating Form for Cultural Knowledge[a]

Student Name: Date:			
	Know it well	I know some	I have no clue
I know the essential norms of culture. (e.g., greetings, dress, behaviors, etc.)			
I know the essential taboos of culture			
I could cite important historical factors that shape culture			
I could cite important socio-political factors that shape culture			
I could describe interactional behaviors common among people in social areas (e.g., family roles, friendship)			
I could describe interactional behaviors common among people in professional areas (e.g., team work, problem solving, etc.)			
I know the education system			
I know the religious practices			
I know the conventions of daily life			
I know historical relations between Turkey and Germany.			
I know the current relations between Turkey and German.			

[a] Adapted from Intercultural Communication Competence Questionnaire (Bektaş-Çetinkaya & Börkan, 2012).

(Rosenberg, 1998, p. 249). Attitude, belief, interest, value, and motivations are among affective traits. In a classroom setting, affective traits of students can be measured with essay type items or performance assessment (teacher's observation while students engage with a task) as with the measurement of knowledge and skills. However, these methods are not really efficient way to measure affective traits for teachers. Construction of a task to elicit student's affective traits is very challenging or in many times not plausible under the given conditions. Hence, self-report measurement, which are an efficient way to measure affective traits, are preferred in spite of limitations inherent in self-report measurements.

An interview and a scale are the two commons techniques of getting self-report measures. Teachers can use personal or group interviews to measures students' affective traits in their classrooms. Teachers may consider advantages and disadvantages of interview technique – but are not limited to: in face to face interviews, teachers have a chance to clarify questions if needed and direct probing question where clarification is needed for students' responses. However, some students may not be comfortable to express their thoughts and feeling in one on one interviews or in the group, or some students may dominate group interviews so others cannot be heard by the teacher.

Self-administered self-report scales measuring attitudes, interest, belief and many other psychological constructs such as depression and anxiety are rarely used by teachers. Developing and administering a scale requires specific skills, knowledge, and expertise. Therefore, it is best to use an existing valid and reliable scales. Four scales measuring affective traits in intercultural competence are given below. In fact, these self-report scales include items measuring more than affective traits. For example, some of them measure self-report knowledge and skills as well. It is note that measuring self-report knowledge and skills is beyond this chapter. Therefore, example items measuring only an affective trait in the scales are provided below.

Assessing Intercultural Competence: Fantini (n.d.)

Please respond to the questions in each of the four categories below, using the scale from 0 (=Not at all) to 5 (= Extremely High). Mark each item TWICE: First, mark with an (X) to indicate your ability at the BEGINNING of your stay in Ecuador. Then, mark the same item with an (X) to indicate your ability at the END of your stay. This will provide a basis for comparison BEFORE and AFTER.

While in Ecuador, I demonstrated willingness to

12. interact with host culture members (I didn't avoid them or primarily seek out my compatriots)	0	1	2	3	4	5
13. learn from my hosts, their language, and their culture	0	1	2	3	4	5
14. try to communicate in Spanish and behave in "appropriate" ways, as judged by my hosts	0	1	2	3	4	5
15. deal with my emotions and frustrations with the host culture (in addition to the pleasures it offered)	0	1	2	3	4	5

Intercultural Sensitivity Scale: G-M. Chen and W. J. Starosta, 2000

5-point scale (1 = strongly disagree to 5 = strongly agree)

1. I enjoy interacting with people from different cultures.   1   2   3   4   5
2. I think people from other cultures are narrow-minded.   1   2   3   4   5
3. I am pretty sure of myself in interacting with people from different cultures.   1   2   3   4   5
4. I find it very hard to talk in front of people from different cultures.   1   2   3   4   5
5. I always know what to say when interacting with people from different cultures.   1   2   3   4   5
6. I can be as sociable as I want to be when interacting with people from different cultures.   1   2   3   4   5
7. I don't like to be with people from different cultures.   1   2   3   4   5
8. I respect the values of people from different cultures   1   2   3   4   5

Cultural Intelligence Scale: L. Van Dyne, S. Ang, and C. Koh, 2009

Read each statement and select the response that best describes your capabilities. Select the answer that BEST describes you AS YOU REALLY ARE (1 = strongly disagree; 7 = strongly agree)

Motivational CQ

1. I enjoy interacting with people from different cultures.   1   2   3   4   5   6   7
2. I am confident that I can socialize with locals in a culture that is unfamiliar to me.
3. I am sure I can deal with the stresses of adjusting to a culture that is new to me.
4. I enjoy living in cultures that are unfamiliar to me.
5. I am confident that I can get accustomed to the shopping conditions in a different culture.

Cross-Cultural Competence Inventory: K. G. Ross, C. A. Thornson, D. P. McDonald and M. C. Arrastia, 2009.

Willingness to Engage 6-point scale (1 = strongly disagree to 6 = strongly agree)

1. I would enjoy visiting other cultures that are unfamiliar to me.   1   2   3   4   5   6

2. If I see someone I know, I usually stop and talk to them.	1	2	3	4	5	6	
3. Traveling to other countries is something I would enjoy.	1	2	3	4	5	6	
4. I enjoy presenting to a group of friends.	1	2	3	4	5	6	
5. I seek opportunities to speak with individuals from other cultural or ethnic backgrounds about their experiences.	1	2	3	4	5	6	
6. I tend to start conversations with strangers like people in the check-out line at the store or beside me on an airplane.	1	2	3	4	5	6	
7. I enjoy talking in a large meeting of friends and acquaintances.	1	2	3	4	5	6	
8. I would enjoy interacting with people from different cultures.	1	2	3	4	5	6	

References

Airasian, P., & Russell, M. (2008). *Classroom assessment: Concepts and applications*. Boston: McGraw-Hill Higher Education.

Albanese, M. A., & Sabers, D. L. (1988). Multiple true-false items: A study of interitem correlations, scoring alternatives, and reliability estimation. *Journal of Educational Measurement, 25*(2), 111–123.

Arter, J. A., & Spandel, V. (1992). Using portfolios of student work in instruction and assessment. *Educational Measurement: Issues and Practice, 11*(1), 36–44.

Bachman, L., & Damböck, B. (2018). *Language assessment for classroom teachers*. Oxford: Oxford University Press.

Bektas-Cetinkaya, Y., & Börkan, B. (2012). Intercultural communicative competence of preservice language teachers in Turkey. In Y. Bayyurt & Y. Bektas-Cetinkaya (Eds.), *Research perspectives on teaching and learning English in Turkey* (pp. 107–119). Frankfurt am Main: Peter Lang.

Belgrad, S. (2013). Portfolios and e-portfolios: Student reflection, self-assessment, and goal setting in the learning process. In J. H. McMillian (Ed.), *Sage handbook of research on classroom assessment* (pp. 331–346). Thousand Oaks, CA: SAGE.

Black, P., Harrison, C., Lee, C., Marshall, B., & Wiliam, D. (2004). Working inside the black box: Assessment for learning in the classroom. *Phi delta kappan, 86*(1), 8–21.

Brookhart, S. M. (2013). *How to create and use rubrics for formative assessment and grading*. Alexandrea: ASCD.

Brown, G. T. L., & Harris, L R. 2013. Student self-assessment. In J. H. McMillian (Ed.), *Sage handbook of research on classroom assessment* (pp. 367–393). Thousand Oaks, CA: SAGE.

Chen, G.-M., & Starosta, W. J. (2000). *The development and validity of the Intercultural Sensitivity Scale.* Paper presented at the annual meeting of National Communication Association, Seattle, WA.

Fantini. (n.d.). Assessing intercultural competence. A Research Project of the Federation EIL Survey Questionnaire Form Alumni. Retrieved April 2, 2020, from http://digitalcollections.sit.edu/cgi/viewcontent.cgi?filename=6&article =1001&context=worldlearning_publications&type=additional.

Hancock, G. R., Thiede, K. W., Sax, G., & Michael, W. B. (1993). Reliability of comparably written two-option multiple-choice and true-false test items. *Educational and Psychological Measurement, 53*(3), 651–660.

Hopkins, K. D. (1998). *Educational and psychological measurement and evaluation.* Needham Heights, MA: Allyn & Bacon.

Hughes, A. (2003). *Testing for language teachers.* Cambridge: Cambridge University Press.

McMillan, J. H. (2007). Formative classroom assessment: The key to improving student achievement. In J. H. McMillan (Ed.), *Formative classroom assessment: Theory into practice* (pp. 1–7). New York: Teachers College Press.

Moss, C. M., & Brookhart, S. M. (2009). *Advancing formative assessment in every classroom: A guide for instructional leaders.* Alexandria, VA: ASCD.

Nitko, A. J., & Brookhart, S. M. (2007). *Education assessment of students.* Upper Sadle River, NJ: Pearson Merrill Prentice Hall.

Ramaprasad, A. (1983). On the definition of feedback. *Behavioral Science, 28*(1), 4–13.

Reynolds, C. R., Livingston, R. B., & Wilson, V. (2006). *Measurement and evaluation in education.* Upper Sadle River, NJ: Pearson Merrill Prentice Hall.

Rosenberg, E. L. (1998). Levels of analysis and the organization of affect. *Review of General Psychology, 2,* 247–270.

Ross, K. G., Thornson, C. A., McDonald, D. P., & Arrastia, M. C. (2009). *The development of the CCCI: The cross-cultural competence inventory.* Patrick AFB, FL: Defense Equal Opportunity Management Institute.

Russell, M. K., & Airasian, P. W. (2008). *Classroom assessment: Concepts and applications.* Boston: McGraw-Hill.

Sadler, D. R. (1989). Formative assessment and the design of instructional systems. *Instructional Science, 18*(2), 119–144.

Sax, G. (1997). *Principles of educational and psychological measurement and evaluation.* Belmont, CA: Wadsworth Publishing.

Van Dyne, L., Ang, S., & Koh, C. (2009). Cultural intelligence: Measurement and scale development. In Moodian, M. (Ed.), *Contemporary leadership and intercultural competence: Exploring the cross-cultural dynamics within organizations* (pp. 233–254). Thousand Oaks, CA: Sage Publications.

Tarkan Kaçmaz

10 Conflict Resolution in Intercultural Communications

The farthest distance is not Africa,
Not India, nor China.
Not even the planets,
Nor the stars that shine at nights.
The farthest distance is between two minds
that fail to understand each other.

Herman Amato

Conflict is a natural and unavoidable part of our lives. Individuals constantly experience and handle conflicts of some sort on interpersonal, intergroup, organizational, societal or even national levels. Even though the word conflict often has negative connotations, conflict itself is not inherently destructive, abnormal or dysfunctional (Moore, 2014). Furthermore, conflicts and disputes may even provide opportunities for growth and socialization. In fact, more than the existence of conflicts, or lack thereof, how they are managed or handled determines the outcome.

Conflict is commonly defined as "an expressed struggle between at least two *interdependent* parties who perceive *incompatible goals*, *scarce resources*, and *interference* from the other party in achieving their goals" (Wilmot & Hocker, 2017). Interdependence refers to a connection or relationship between the parties who may rely on one another for a mutually desired outcome. Incompatible goals include different methods or approaches towards an otherwise common goal. Scarce resources and sharing them in an equal and fair manner potentially cause problems, and finally, interference is other party's posing a threat against achieving one's goals.

Conflicts can escalate simply from varying personalities and perspectives and become conflicts if not properly handled earlier in the progression of conflict. Fig. 1 below illustrates Conflict Escalation.

Along this continuum, parties communicate and address their differences and negotiate a mutually satisfying amicable solution, but when negotiations do not yield desired results and simple differences of opinion reach the level of conflict

CONFLICT ESCALATION

| Varying personalities and perspectivies | Differences of opinion | Disagreement | Dispute | Conflict |

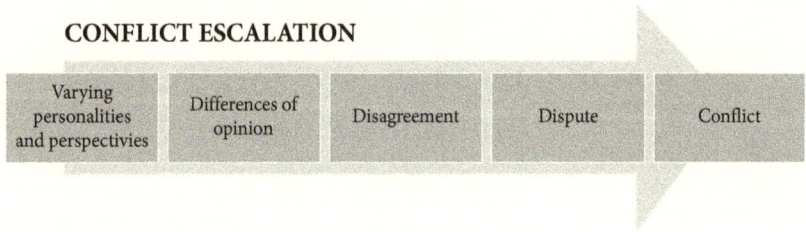

Fig. 1: Conflict Escalation

they can rarely be resolved by the parties involved and may require a third party's involvement because human nature and psychological defense mechanisms usually render parties adamant to recognize, admit or accept the merits of the other party's arguments. Parties often tend to firmly adhere to their position – not aware of the underlying needs and interests that put them in that position in the first place.

In the last several decades, traditional approaches to conflicts such as legal and judicial procedures and administrative decision or arbitration have begun to be replaced by more private decision-making processes such as negotiation and mediation. Alternative Dispute Resolution (ADR) is one such approach to conflict that mainly consists of back-and-forth communication designed to reach an agreement (Fisher & Ury, 2011). Especially in individualistic societies such as Western Europe and North America where everyone wants to participate in decisions that affect them; fewer and fewer people will accept decisions dictated by someone else. For instance, the US Department of Justice reports that in 2017, almost 80 % of the conflicts were resolved through ADR procedures, both voluntary and court-ordered (USDOJ, 2017). In more collectivist societies, such as Turkey, people tend to trust and rely more on external decision-making processes such that are provided by the intervention and ruling of an authority, usually legal or judicial. However, the Turkish Ministry of Justice initiated an Alternative Dispute Resolution department, necessary amendments in the penal code were made and several laws and regulations on the processes and procedures went into effect in the last decade (Ministry of Justice Alternative Dispute Resolution and Mediation Directorates).

Conflict Resolution Process

Managing conflict effectively is a simple two-step process that starts with "how we assess the conflict we're facing", followed by "what action (or inaction) we decide to take to address it" (Furlong, 2005). The first step in conflict resolution, obviously, is negotiation where parties discuss their differences, voice their concerns, express their feelings and emotions, try to understand the impact and consequences of their actions and attempt to arrive at a mutually acceptable and satisfying resolution. Nevertheless, conflicts cannot always be resolved through negotiation alone and when conflict escalates and parties are not able to resolve it through negotiation, involvement, and intervention of a third party is often necessary, as Albert Einstein once said: "Problems cannot be solved with the same mindset that created them". The third party—the mediator, in this process—is an impartial, unbiased party who facilitates the negotiations between conflicting parties towards a peaceful and mutually acceptable agreement which would restore, repair or, if necessary, end the relationship between the parties while reaching an agreement that satisfies the needs of all involved. Thus, a mediator needs to establish a healthy dialog and keep the communication channels open throughout the process.

In a typical conflict resolution process, the mediator performs a conflict analysis to develop an understanding of the sources and reasons of the conflict by studying the parties involved, the history and the background of the conflict, the issues surrounding the conflict, and the underlying needs and interests of the parties. This analysis starts even before meeting with the parties and continues throughout the course of the mediation. It also requires the mediator to utilize advanced communication skills to understand the dynamics of the conflict and the parties' standpoint. Parties to the conflict usually come to mediation with a fixed position which may or may not reflect their actual needs and interests. As a matter of fact, it is rather difficult to identify those needs and interests as the parties themselves may not be aware of them. Instead, they stick to a position under the circumstances that they created and try to standby that position.

The relationship between positions and needs and interests is often portrayed using "iceberg" or "onion" metaphors. The position (what the parties say they want) is represented by the tip of the iceberg and the aptly named underlying needs and interests (what parties really want and what motivates them) are represented by its body underwater. The tip of the iceberg metaphor is, indeed, very illustrative of such comparison due to the sheer size difference and the ratio of the parts of the iceberg's mass. The onion model is also a useful one to illustrate that relationship. The onion has a rough outer skin on the surface which is readily visible but not necessarily useful and of any value. Beneath that outer skin, as you start to peel deeper into the rings, you reach the bud of the onion. It is elemental that the underlying needs and interests be identified during conflict resolution process if the conflict is to be resolved, otherwise, the process turns into bargaining or haggling over positions and preferred solutions of each party, not addressing and fulfilling the actual needs and interests of the parties, and, hence, cannot bear win-win results. The positions people bring to the table usually happen to be unrealistic, unreasonable, untenable, even vindictive and spiteful. Communication plays a key role in helping parties become aware of the needs and interests of the other party—and their own, and continue to work together towards a mutually acceptable and satisfactory solution to their conflict.

In the "reaching an agreement stage" of conflict resolution process, parties need to determine their BATNA's (Best Alternative to a Negotiated Agreement) which basically means the best alternative solution if the one they originally proposed is not possible. Helping parties understand the dynamics of the conflict, communicate with the other party, make informed decisions, evaluate their settlement options and compare them to their BATNA's usually leads to successful conflict resolution. Identifying BATNA's is an important and necessary skill for the parties in the conflict resolution process and as with all other aspects of conflict resolution, solid communication skills such as self-expression and active listening play a key role. For a successful conflict resolution process parties need to be ready and willing to compromise their position and settle for their BATNA's to avoid an impasse. Parties may need to do a reality test and reiterate their options. This reality test involves discussing the potential results and consequences if parties remain adamant to reconsider their positions and make concessions if necessary. They may have to review and revise their BATNA's and those of the other party's. Agreement and resolution will only be possible if and when both parties' BATNA's overlap at least minimally, which is called ZOPA (Zone of Proximal Agreement). On the other hand, if either party's BATNA fails to meet their reservation point the process ends without agreement.

Approaches to Conflict and Outcomes

Parties' approach to conflict and procedures and strategies used to handle conflict determine the type outcome achieved. Johnson and Johnson (1996) posit that there are two major concerns in conflict resolution: (a) concern about reaching one's goals and (b) concern about maintaining an appropriate relationship with the other party. In order to address those concerns they list five strategies toward resolution: (a) *integrative*, win-win problem-solving negotiations by which an agreement is sought that ensures that both parties fully achieve their goals and that any tensions and negative feelings are resolved; (b) *compromise* in which the disputants give up part of their goals and sacrifice part of the relationship in order to reach an agreement; (c) *smoothing* in which the disputant gives

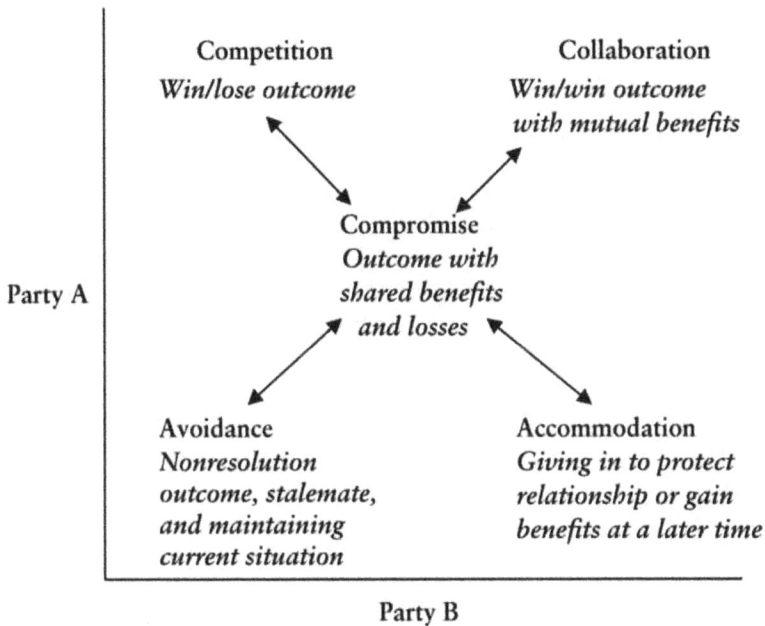

Fig. 2: Conflict Approaches, Strategies, and Outcomes (Adapted from Moore, 2014)

up his or her goals in order to maintain the relationship at the highest quality possible); (d) **withdrawing** in which the disputant gives up both the goal and the relationship and avoids the issue and the other person; and (e) **forcing** or distributive, win-lose negotiations in which the disputant seeks to achieve his or her goal by forcing or persuading the other to yield (Johnson & Johnson, 1995). The most sought-after resolution type, naturally, is the win/win outcome which satisfies both parties' needs and interests to a certain degree; as opposed to win/lose, lose/lose or stalemate outcomes. Win/win outcomes require collaboration which can only be possible through healthy and sustained communication. Lack of adequate communication likely results in an overly competitive process and usually leads to win/lose outcome. On the other hand, avoidance or accommodation strategies may lead to stalemate outcomes or no resolution (See Fig. 2).

Communication Skills in Conflict Resolution

Communication is the lifeblood of any conflict resolution process. Failed communication or miscommunication jeopardizes the success of any conflict

resolution process as communication barriers may hinder coding/decoding processes which leads to misunderstandings or misinformation. An obvious issue
in communication among cultures is language. Even when people from two
cultures appear to speak the same language, regional and national differences
may cause confusion. More important than these minor differences is the difficulty of communicating when the parties do not speak the same language, and
even if one of the parties has learned the other's language, miscommunication
can occur. (Moore & Woodrow, 2010).

In order to reach agreements, parties must communicate and exchange information with each other and be able to accurately interpret and understand data
that have been presented and they need to be able to exchange information on
their feelings, perceptions, concerns, interests, needs, goals, objectives, visions,
and procedural preferences (Moore & Woodrow, 2010). Good communication is considered to be central for productive conflict resolution. According
to Wilmot and Hocker (2017), communication and conflict are related in the
following ways:

- Communication behavior often creates conflict.
- Communication behavior reflects conflict.
- Communication is the vehicle for the productive or destructive management
  of conflict.

A typical conflict resolution process involves addressing the issues and concerns,
exploring the history and sources of conflict, identifying the underlying needs
and interests, understanding the social structures and power dynamics and,
finally, negotiating a mutually acceptable amicable agreement towards solving
the dispute, all of which rely on effective communication (See Fig. 3). Parties
need to be equipped with and utilize a set of effective communication skills in
order to move further in the conflict resolution process.

The conflict resolution process may come to a halt if participants fail to speak
and listen to one another and gain a close approximation of each other's meaning
and intent (Moore & Woodrow, 2010). This becomes even more difficult in intercultural contexts mainly due to language difference. Understanding someone
from our own culture speaking our native language may be painstakingly hard.
This difficulty is magnified with people who come from different cultures and are
not native speakers of the language (Moore & Woodrow, 2010). Understanding
the culture as well as the language competence and proficiency is also at play here
as language, to a large extent, affects individuals' way of thinking. Therefore, it
is not unusual for parties to reach an impasse in negotiations, or encounter any
one of a wide range of problems related to miscommunication. For that reason,

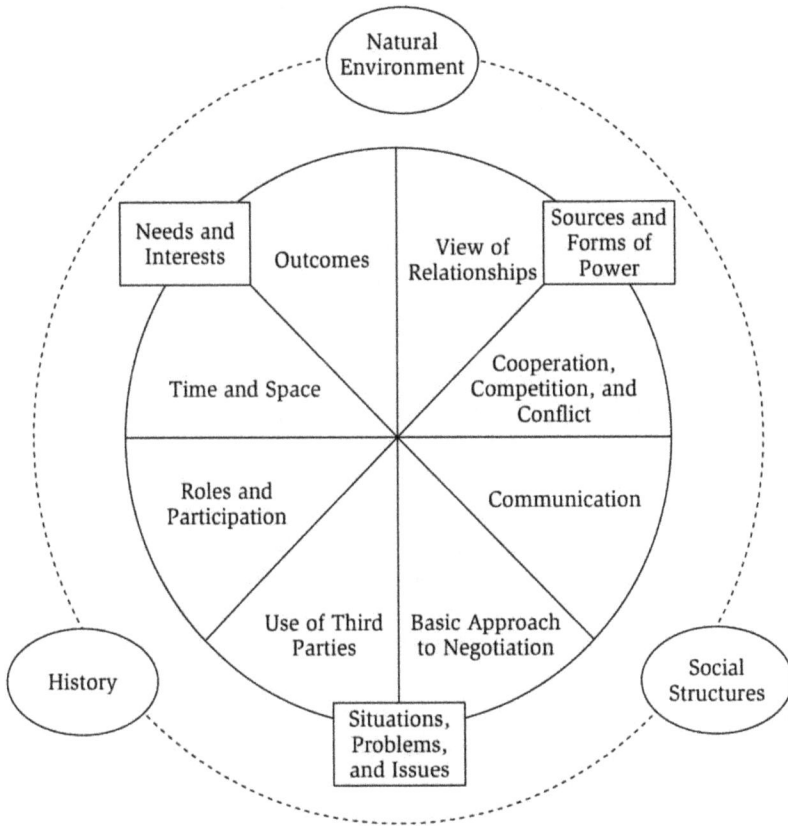

Fig. 3: Sources of Conflict (Adapted from Moore & Woodrow, 2010)

conflict resolution and mediation programs almost always include improved interpersonal communication skills (Johnson & Johnson, 1996). Placing socially unskilled individuals in a group and telling them to cooperate does not guarantee that they will be able to do so effectively, therefore, leadership, decision-making, trust-building, communication, and conflict-management skills must be taught the just as purposefully and precisely as academic skills (Johnson & Johnson, 1995). Lack of adequate communication skills may lead to communication barriers such as misunderstandings, inability to express oneself, and lack of empathy which need to be addressed properly before they mar the communication and jeopardize the conflict resolution process.

Communication skills that are relevant to effective interpersonal communication and conflict management include self-disclosure, explaining, active listening, perspective taking, reframing, and brainstorming (Deutsch, 2000). In several recent studies, inadequate communication, inability to express oneself, inconsistency in statements, inability to empathize, and difficulty understanding other's perspective were found to be the most common problems disputants encountered in conflict resolution process (Kaçmaz, 2011; Kaçmaz & Türnüklü, 2011). Successful, effective and sustained communication requires several skills that include, among others, active listening, effective questioning, empathy, reflection, rephrasing, reframing, etc.

Self-expression/self-disclosure: In order to establish and maintain a healthy communication channel parties need to be able to clearly express their feelings and emotions and needs and interests. The first step in accomplishing that is to separate the people from the problems. Dwelling on specific attitudes and behavior by the other party almost always is counterproductive. The process may quickly turn into a blame game or name-calling and psychological defense mechanisms may kick in which usually causes parties to firmly standby their position and fail to see the merits of the other party's arguments. One good strategy is to refrain from suggesting or assigning blame or making accusatory comments. Using "*I-messages*" instead of "*You-messages*" would still convey the same information and help avoid defensive or hostile reaction. Focusing on feelings and emotions caused by the behavior rather than the behavior itself may help uncover underlying needs and interests. Throughout the process foul, demeaning, condescending, derogatory and flaming language should also be avoided.

Active Listening: Purpose of active listening is to put forth the effort to try to understand what the other party is really saying through their words, thoughts and feelings as expressed by actual words, verbal and non-verbal clues, tone of voice and body language. Parties often tend to mask their thoughts and feelings until they are acknowledged and appreciated by the other party. Providing feedback is frequently utilized in active listening, although patronizing comments should be avoided. Also, waiting until the other party finishes their sentence just to comment on what is being said or follow with a rebuttal is not active listening, and in fact, counterproductive. If a party is already contemplating on what to say next before the other party finishes her/his sentence, it is not really listening but waiting for the turn to speak. As the American educator and author Stephen R. Covey eloquently puts it as "The biggest communication problem is we do not listen to understand. We listen to reply". Hence, speaking in turns does not necessarily ensure successful communication.

Effective Questioning: Asking questions is another important skill in communication. Asking the right questions could elicit the right answers and provide much-needed information regarding the conflict towards understanding the nature and causes of conflict. Asking good questions and actively and effectively listening to the answers are crucial skills for a working dialog.

Although close-ended, Yes/No questions might prove useful in the initial stages of communication, open-ended questions provide more information, especially those which start with "What" and "How" instead of "Why", because "Why" questions may potentially result in justification and defense instead of information and clarification. Even some "What" and "How" questions may sometimes elicit simple one-word answers. In such cases, focal point or wording of the question may need to be altered or follow-up questions may be asked. For example, the following question may potentially yield a short answer and may need to be rephrased to elicit more information or a follow-up question may be asked:

Q: What did you think of this piece?
A: Great!
Q: What would you need us to change about this piece?
A: ....

Open-ended question types may include, among others, information-gathering, explanatory, clarifying, expanding, reflective, creative, focusing, challenging, funneling, rhetorical, conclusive, etc. Tab. 1 adapted from Moore (2014) lists some of these types of questions and provides the goals and purposes and examples for those question types which may help maintain effective communication and elicit necessary information in a conflict resolution process.

Empathy Skills: Empathy allows conflicting parties to develop an understanding of the impact of the conflict on the parties' feelings and emotions and share them. It may be difficult for individuals to empathize with the other party for it seemingly involves admission of wrong-doing or unconditional acceptance of the merits of others' arguments. Empathy skills may be partly innate and partly learned. This means they can be developed or improved. The ability to empathize is often associated with social skills that motivate altruistic and prosocial behavior (McDonald & Messinger, 2011). Although empathy skills, to a large extent, develop during the early years of life, individuals may be encouraged to exhibit empathetic behavior through communication skills that promote understanding and perspective taking.

Tab. 1: Types of Questions (adapted from Moore, 2014)

Type of Question	Purpose or Goal of Question	Example
Closed or Narrowing Question	• To narrow the range of possible responses by a party and limit the kind of information given • To get a party to be more specific • To get a yes or no answer	• *When exactly did the problem begin to develop?* • *Did you disagree with the proposal?* • *Did he or she follow through on the commitment?*
Clarifying Question	• To elicit more information when the topic is complex or the mediator is confused • To clarify a specific point • To confirm understanding • To move from general information to specifics	• *I'm a bit confused about that point; could you clarify it for me?* • *Could I get a bit more detail about your proposal so that I can better understand your thinking and goals?* • *I think I understand what you have said. (Repeat the understanding.) Is this right?*
Broadening or Expanding Question	• To get a more complete picture of a situation or problem • To encourage a party to elaborate on a point • To expand possible issues, needs, or interests that can be used to find an acceptable agreement	• *What else occurred that made you see the situation in that way?* • *What other factors should be considered?* • *What other interests are important to you and your organization?*
Explaining Question	• To elicit more information on the reasoning behind a party's perspective, view, or position • To encourage greater introspection	• *What makes this so important to you?* • *How did you decide about what should be done?* • *What questions did what happen raise for you?*

Tab. 1: Continued

Type of Question	Purpose or Goal of Question	Example
Interest-Based Question	• To elicit and clarify psychological and relationship interests • To elicit and clarify procedural interests • To elicit and clarify substantive interests	• *What concerns do you have about . . .?* • *How did you feel about what happened?* • *How would you like to feel in the future?* • *What kind of relationship do you want in the future?* • *What about the process was a problem?* • *What process would you like to use to settle this issue?* • *What is most important for you to achieve in the settlement of this issue?*
Challenging Question	• To challenge or confront a respondent's reasoning or logic • To elicit or demonstrate contradictions in logic or intended outcomes • To encourage a change of mind	• *Can you explain to me what seems to be a difference between your past and current actions?* • *Can you explain your thinking, because I just don't get it?* • *Can you show me how this would really work and how it meets either of our interests?*
Option Generation Question	• To encourage a respondent to think about or develop multiple options • To frame option generation in terms of meeting joint goals or interests	• *What could be done to better achieve your goals and meet your interests?* • *Do you see two or three ways that we might address our concerns, achieve our goals, and meet our interests?* • *How might we do that? Can you think of some ways?*
Consequential Question	• To encourage a realistic assessment of future consequences, costs, or benefits of an action or agreement	• *What might happen if . . .?* • *How might you or others feel about . . .?* • *So what might happen if we do that?* • *Are there any costs or downsides of that option in the future?* • *Are there potential benefits of that option for either of you in the future?* • *Do you really think that you can win (in court)?* • *What will this option really cost?*

Reflection: Individuals may be encouraged to reflect on their actions and the potential impact of their actions on others' feelings and emotions through self-expression, self-disclosure, and critical thinking.

Rephrasing/paraphrasing/summarizing: For clarification and confirmation purposes and to enhance understanding, individuals' statements may be rephrased, paraphrased or summarized using different words or expressions.

Reframing: Framing focuses and accentuates an idea or opinion from a certain perspective which may, at times, fail to get the right message across if the other party has a varied take on the issues and look at things from a different perspective. In such instances, reframing the statement/idea/opinion may be called for. Reframing the issue from a different perspective sometimes enables the other party to actually see the merits of the other party's argument. Reframing can be achieved using various methods such as reframing damaging, negative, judgmental or poisonous language; redefining the conceptualization of the conflict; reframing the issues using metaphors that can be more easily understood by the parties.

Reframing can also be achieved by "enlarging the cake" so that everyone gets what they perceive to be an equal slice of the cake. In a TEDx speech, the author of "Getting to Yes" William Ury retells a well-known children's story about a man who leaves his 17 camels to his sons as inheritance:

A father left 17 camels to his three sons as inheritance.

The will of the father stated that the eldest son should get half of 17 camels,

The middle son should be given 1/3 of 17 camels,

Youngest son should be given 1/9 of the 17 camels.

As it is not possible to divide 17 into half or by 3 or 9, the sons started to fight with each other.

How can the sons divide the camels among themselves?

The sons decided to go to a wise man to solve this issue. The wise man listened patiently, and after giving this thought, brought one camel of his own and added it to 17. Now they had 18 camels.

Half of 18 = 9. So, he gave 9 camels to the eldest son.

1/3 of 18 = 6. So, he gave 6 camels to the middle son.

1/9 of 18 = 2.. So, he gave camels to the youngest son.

9 + 6 + 2 = 17 and the wise man took his camel back.

As a matter of fact, 17 is a prime number which is only divisible by 1 and itself. The 18th camel here served as the common ground or the catalyst. What the wise man did here was to think outside the box and enlarge the cake so each son got their inheritance, at least on principle. Thinking outside the box, a term actually created by business management consultants in 1980s and 1990s, is a metaphor used to encourage people to look at things from a different perspective, outside the boundaries of conventional and traditional wisdom which may limit our problem-solving capacity because of our tendency to comply with perceived set rules and fixed train of thought. Through well-orchestrated communication, parties to the conflict can be encouraged to come up with more ways to solve their conflict and avoid an impasse.

Implications for Language Learning

Conflict resolution processes heavily utilize good communication skills. Language competence seems to be one of the significant factors determining the success or failure of conflict resolution processes. Helping learners develop effective communication skills will empower them to become good negotiators in resolving their own conflicts. It may also help them become good mediators helping other individuals negotiate their conflicts. The communication skills listed in earlier sections of the chapter will need to be emphasized where possible, especially in oral communications and related courses. Debates, dialogs, presentations and similar activities may help learners develop their communication skills.

Conflict resolution and peer-mediation programs in schools were found to also serve that purpose (Johnson & Johnson, 1995). A study on the perspectives of peer mediators receiving such training revealed that the peer-mediators believed the conflict resolution and peer-mediation program they received helped them become better communicators; their self-esteem and self-confidence improved, and they were able to help others establish and maintain effective communication during the conflict resolution processes (Kaçmaz, 2011).

Oral Communications courses could also include exercises and activities that focus on and help learners develop these effective communication and negotiation skills. Sample cases like the following scenario could be used to illustrate and raise awareness of the effectiveness and importance of good communication and negotiation skills:

Sample Conflict

> Imagine for a moment that you are faced with a conflict.
> Imagine, for example, that your new neighbor loves to
> have guests over many nights of the week until the early
> hours of the morning, keeping you up with the noise.
> When you talk to your neighbor, he laughs and tells you,
> "Loosen up, have some fun. Come and join us if you
> want! You need to enjoy life more!" You go home after
> the conversation and get increasingly angry. You think
> about how insensitive he is, how little he cares for other
> people. Given how you see the problem, you vow to call
> the police the next time he has a party during the week.
> *(adapted from Furlong, 2005)*

This conflict is headed for a significant escalation if not handled properly. This could go one of two ways. You can either confront your neighbor, exchange a few unpleasantries, maybe insert some slurs and finish with a threat to call the police and file a complaint which would likely end your nodding acquaintance; or you can have a productive conversation with your neighbor which utilizes the communication skills listed earlier and maybe even become and remain good neighbors:

Neighbor#1 – Hello neighbor! Sorry to interrupt. Just came by to let you know that I have an early start tomorrow and I have trouble going to sleep when there is a lot of noise past midnight. It's already hard for me to do that what with my recent bout of insomnia and panic attack episodes.

Neighbor#2 – This is my apartment and I have the right to socialize and have some fun every now and then.

Neighbor#1 – I totally understand you are entitled to have fun at your apartment but I'm sure you would agree these buildings are hardly sound proof and believe me when I say that the noise is almost amplified by these thin walls.

Neighbor#2 – Well, tough. The music stays on.

Neighbor#1 – Oh, I'm not asking you to turn it off. I love listening to music, myself. Could you maybe consider switching to easy listening music after late hours?

Neighbor#2 – Well, I guess I can do that. Sorry for the trouble.

Neighbor#1 – Thanks, that's very kind of you. Good night and have fun.

Similar cases may be used as part of an Oral Communications course, for instance, where learners may be assigned roles and asked to act out the conversation or mediate the conflict paying attention to the communication and negotiation skills. This role-play activity may provide them the opportunity to practice these skills and use them in resolving conflicts.

Finally, it is apparent that language teaching programs will need to be revised and redesigned to include, focus on and emphasize effective communication and negotiation skills which, especially in these trying times shifting paradigms, individuals rely more on than ever before.

References

Deutsch, M. (2000). Cooperation and conflict. In M. Deutsch & P. Coleman (Eds.), *The handbook of conflict resolution* (pp. 21 – 40). San Francisco, CA: Jossey-Bass.

Fisher, R., & Ury, P. (2011). *Getting to Yes: Negotiating agreement without giving in.* (Ed. Patton, B.) New York: Penguin.

Furlong, G. T. (2005). *The conflict resolution toolbox: Models and maps for analyzing, diagnosing and resolving conflict.* Ontario: Wiley & Sons.

Johnson, D. W., & Johnson, R. T. (1995). *Reducing school violence through conflict resolution.* Alexandria, VA: Association for Supervision and Curriculum Development.

Johnson, D. W., & Johnson, R. T. (1996). Conflict resolution and peer mediation programs in elementary and secondary schools: A review of the research. *Review of Educational Research, 66*(4), 459–506. https://doi. org/10.3102/00346543066004459

Kaçmaz, T. (2011). Perspectives of primary school peer mediators on their mediation practices. *Egitim Arastirmalari-Eurasian Journal of Educational Research, 43,* 125–142.

Kaçmaz, T., & Türnüklü, A. (2011). Akran Arabulucularin Perspektifinden Çatisan Ögrencilerin Arabuluculuk Sürecinde Yasadigi Zorluklar. *Ilkögretim Online, 10*(3), 798–812. [Online]: http://ilkogretim-online.org. tr.

McDonald, N. M., & Messinger, D. S. (2011). The development of empathy: How, when, and why. In J. J. Sanguineti, A. Acerbi, & J. A. Lombo (Eds.), *Moral behavior and free will: A neurobiological and philosophical approach* (pp. 341–368) Vatican City: IF Press.

Ministry of Justice, Alternative Dispute Resolution Directorate, Ceza Muhakemesinde Uzlaştırma Yönetmeliği. http://alternatifcozumler.adalet. gov.tr/Resimler/Mevzuat/312020115054uzla%C5%9Ft%C4%B1rma%20 y%C3%B6netmeli%C4%9Fi.pdf (accessed on 25 December 2019).

Ministry of Justice, Mediation Directorate, 6325 sayılı Hukuk Uyuşmazlıklarında Arabuluculuk Kanunu, https://www.mevzuat.gov.tr/MevzuatMetin/1.5.6325.pdf (accessed on 25 December 2019).

Moore, C. W. (2014). *The mediation process: Practical strategies for resolving conflict* (4th ed.). San Francisco: Jossey-Bass.

Moore, C. W., & Woodrow, P. J. (2010). *Handbook of global and multicultural negotiation*. San Francisco: Jossey-Bass.

USDOJ Fiscal Year Report 2017. Use and Benefits of ADR https://www.justice.gov/olp/alternative-dispute-resolution-department-justice (accessed 31 January 2020.

Wilmot, W. W., & Hocker, J. L. (2017). *Interpersonal conflict* (10th ed.). New York: McGraw-Hill.

Contributors

Deren Başak Akman Yeşilel (deren.akman@omu.edu.tr) received her M.A. degree from Ondokuz Mayıs University. She held a Ph.D. in the area of English Language Education from Gazi University in 2012. She currently works at Ondokuz Mayıs University, Department of Foreign Languages Education. She has many distinguished studies in the areas of teaching English to young learners, technology and language learning, materials development and teacher training.

Arda Arikan (ardaari@gmail.com) Graduating from Hacettepe University, Faculty of Letters, Department of American Culture and Literature in 1996, and continuing his MA thesis in the same department. Prof. Dr. Arikan completed his PhD at Penn State University in Language, Culture, and Society program in 2002. In 2010, he received the title of associate professor in the field of English Language Education and became a full professor in September 2016. He is currently employed at Akdeniz University, Faculty of Letters, Department of English Language and Literature. He continues his scientific studies as a generalist by reading and writing on education, literature, and culture.

Asuman Aşık (asuman.asik@gazi.edu.tr) is a faculty member of the Department of English Language Teaching at Gazi University, Turkey. She received her bachelor's degree from the Department of English Language and Literature, Hacettepe University, MA and PhD degree from the Department of English Language Teaching, Gazi University, Turkey. Her research interests are corpora and language teaching, classroom discourse, young learners of English, teacher training, materials development, TPACK, technology and language teaching.

Yeşim Bektaş-Çetinkaya (yesim.cetinkaya@deu.edu.tr; yesim.bcetinkaya@gmail.com) is an associate professor in the Department of Foreign Language Education at Dokuz Eylul University in Izmir, Turkey. She has an M.A. and Ph.D. in Foreign Language Education from Ohio State University (USA). Her research interests include intercultural communication, affective variables in foreign language education, teacher education and language literacy. She has published several articles in international journals, book chapters and books.

Esma Biricik Deniz (esmabiricik@gmail.com) has been working as an instructor for ten years in the School of Foreign Languages at Cukurova University, Adana, Turkey. She got her PhD degree in English Language Education at Cukurova

University. Her research interests include pre-service language teacher education, ELF and World Englishes. She has conducted and participated in several projects and research studies on ELF-aware pedagogy and ELF-aware pre-service teacher education. She is also currently carrying out a research study on ELF and teacher education.

Bengü Börkan (bengu.borkan@boun.edu.tr) is an associate professor in the Department of Educational Sciences at Boğaziçi University where she has been a faculty member since 2008. Dr. Börkan completed her master and Ph.D. at the Ohio State University and his undergraduate studies at The Middle East Technical University. Her research interests lie in the area of quantitative research, measurement and evaluation in education. She has collaborated actively with researchers in several other disciplines of guidance and counseling, developmental psychology and adult education as a research methodologist.

Servet Çelik (servet61@trabzon.edu.tr) is an associate professor and head of the Department of Foreign Language Education at Trabzon University, Turkey. He holds a Master of Education degree in TESOL from the University of Pennsylvania, USA, and a doctoral degree in Literacy, Culture and Language Education from Indiana University-Bloomington, USA. Dr. Çelik has been extensively involved in English language curriculum design and teacher professional development through national and international projects, workshops and seminars for EFL teachers in predominantly disadvantaged local contexts, and research particularly on teaching for diversity, intercultural awareness, and the issues surrounding multilingualism and multiculturalism in pluralistic societies. Dr. Çelik currently serves as the executive co-editor of Sustainable Multilingualism (ISSN 2335-2019).

Şakire Erbay Çetinkaya (sakireerbay@ktu.edu.tr) has been working as a lecturer in the department of English Language and Literature at Karadeniz Technical University (KTU). She holds a master's degree in Applied Linguistics and a doctoral degree, also from KTU. She has been teaching various courses on English oracy and literacy, research methods, and BA supervision. Her research interests include the paradigm of English as an International Languages/ELF/WE, culture, instructional materials evaluation and design, reflective practice, and academic writing instruction. She has published articles in various journals such as Education and Science, The Qualitative Report, Reflective Practice, Journal of Further and Higher Education, Turkish Online Journal of Qualitative Inquiry (TOJQI).

Esim Gürsoy (esim@uludag.edu.tr) is a professor at the ELT Department of Bursa Uludağ University, Turkey. She holds an M.A. in teacher education from Ohio University, USA and a Ph.D in English Language Teaching from Anadolu, University, Turkey. She has many published research articles in international journals. She has authored and edited books and also is the author of several book chapters. Her research interests include, teaching English to young learners, pre-service teacher education, teaching practice, and integrating socially responsible teaching to ELT.

Berna Güryay (bernaguryay@gmail.com) is an assistant professor in English Language Teaching Program at Dokuz Eylül University. She has completed her MA and PhD degrees in the same department and has been working there since 2002. She has taught various lessons such as language acquisition, special teaching methods, teaching language skills and drama. Besides, she has presented in several conferences, published articles and book chapters in the ELT area. Her research interests are mainly teacher education, second language acquisition and English language teaching with particular emphasis on creative drama, individual differences and identity.

Tarkan Kaçmaz (tarkan.kacmaz@deu.edu.tr, tkacmaz@gmail.com) is an associate professor in the Department of Foreign Language Education at Dokuz Eylül University, İzmir-Turkey. He received his doctorate in Curriculum & Instruction from Indiana University (USA). His research interests include instructional technology, interpersonal relations, conflict resolution and intercultural communication. He took part in various research projects, authored and co-authored research articles, books, book chapters and reports.

Elif Kemaloglu-Er (ekemalogluer@atu.edu.tr; ekemaloglu@gmail.com) is an assistant professor in the Department of Translation and Interpreting at Adana Alparslan Türkeş Science and Technology University. She received her PhD degree in English Language Education at Bogazici University with her dissertation on ELF-aware pre-service teacher education. Several of her publications focus on ELF-awareness in language teaching and language teacher education and she has been an active participant and a leader in multifaceted ELF-related projects. Her research interests include English language teaching, English language teacher education, ELF and World Englishes.

Claudia Nickolson (Claudia.nickolson@uncp.edu) completed her Master's degree and Ph.D.at the Pennsylvania State University where she divided her time between Language and Literacy Education and Rural Sociology. She is an associate professor of Teacher Education at the University of North Carolina at Pembroke. Her interests intersect in the field of migrant education.

Eda Nur Özcan is an instructor at Bursa Technical University. She has completed her bachelor's degree at Marmara University and she holds a Master's degree from the department of English language and education at Bursa Uludağ University. Her research interests are material development and evaluation, intercultural awareness and global education.

Gonca Yangın Ekşi (goncayangin@gmail.com) is a professor in English Language Teaching (ELT) in the Department of Foreign Language Education, Gazi University. The courses she has offered include Teaching English to Young Learners, Practice Teaching, ICT and CALL, Curriculum development and Materials Evaluation, Language learning theories, and Psychology of the language learner. She received her MA in ELT in Hacettepe University, Department of ELT and she holds her Ph.D. in ELT in Gazi University. She has worked in a number of projects including the national project for the development of the national English curriculum for Primary and Secondary schools. Her research interests include computer-assisted language learning, pre- and in-service teacher education, curriculum and materials development, teaching skills and language components, young learners, use of corpus in language teaching.

Ceylan Yangın Ersanlı (ceylany@omu.edu.tr) obtained her PhD in "English Language Education" at Gazi University in 2010 with her thesis "Developing prospective English language teachers' comprehension of texts with humorous elements". She currently works as an Associate Professor and researcher at the Department of English Language Education at Ondokuz Mayıs University. Her main research interests are teaching English to young learners, curriculum development, CLIL and teacher training.

Mehmet Galip Zorba (galipzorba@akdeniz.edu.tr) Following his M.A, Mehmet Galip Zorba completed his PhD in ELT in 2019. His research interests are cultural issues in ELT, materials evaluation, children's literature and digital literacy. He is currently working at Akdeniz University, English Language and Literature Department.

9783631820148